Poems From The North West

Edited by Claire Tupholme

 Young**Writers**

First published in Great Britain in 2008 by:
Young Writers
Remus House
Coltsfoot Drive
Peterborough
PE2 9JX
Telephone: 01733 890066
Website: www.youngwriters.co.uk

SB ISBN 978-1 84431 503 1

Foreword

Young Writers was established in 1991 and has been passionately devoted to the promotion of reading and writing in children and young adults ever since. The quest continues today. Young Writers remains as committed to the nurturing of poetic and literary talent as ever.

This year's Young Writers competition has proven as vibrant and dynamic as ever and we are delighted to present a showcase of the best poetry from across the UK and in some cases overseas. Each poem has been selected from a wealth of *Little Laureates* entries before ultimately being published in this, our sixteenth primary school poetry series.

Once again, we have been supremely impressed by the overall quality of the entries we have received. The imagination, energy and creativity which has gone into each young writer's entry made choosing the poems a challenging and often difficult but ultimately hugely rewarding task - the general high standard of the work submitted ensured this opportunity to bring their poetry to a larger appreciative audience.

We sincerely hope you are pleased with this final collection and that you will enjoy *Little Laureates Poems From The North West* for many years to come.

Contents

Zoe Higham (8)	39
Molly Wolstenholme (7)	39
Aaron Dunne (8)	40
Benjamin Powell (8)	40
Edward Mooney (7)	41
Luann Jordan Dickson (7)	41
Daniel Evans (8)	42
Reece Hampstead (10)	42
Cameron Thompson (7)	43
Jack Cope (8)	43
Hannah Rachael Costin (11)	44
Rebecca Sarah Large (10)	45
Michael Cope (10)	46
Danielle Cope (10)	47
Alexandra Faulkner (10)	48
Ben Lewis Etchells (9)	49
Kyle Moore (7)	49
Stephen Nevins (8)	50

Longbarn Community Primary School, Warrington

Jack Breary (10)	50
Jake Wall (10)	50
Paul Cordingley (11)	51
Megan Breary (10)	51
Lewis Hanglin (9)	51
Jessica Neild (9)	52
Sam Vernon (10)	52
Charlotte Hulme (10)	53
Dominic McAlinden (10)	53

Lower Park Primary School, Poynton

Liam Johnston (8)	53
Rachel Cunio (10)	54
Georgie Clayton (10)	55
Sophie Hudson & Francesca Parrot	56
Victoria Booth (9)	57
Georgia Clay (10)	58
Tom Holmes (8)	58
Poppy Plumb (10)	59
Alicia Vermeulen (9)	59
Katie Sharrocks (9)	60

Newton Primary School, Chester

Onchan Primary School, Douglas

Hannah Louise Frost (9)	77
Lewis Croft (9)	77
Jonathan Kneale (9)	78
Adam Peet (9)	78

St Brigid's RC Primary School, Knowsley

Lewis Humphreys (7)	79
Aaron Towner (7)	80
Jordanna Shelbourne (7)	81
Erin Ellis (7)	82
Keavy Christian (7)	83
Morgan Povey (8)	84
Mia Grimes (7)	85
Megan Farrington (7)	86

St John's CE Primary School, Sandbach

St John's CE Primary School Book Club	87

SS Peter & Paul RC Primary School, Wallasey

Sean Clarke (10)	88
Josephine Ruiz (9)	88
Hafiza Brepotra (10)	89
Gabriel Pillitteri (9)	89
Alastair Nokes (10)	90
Alexandra Smith (10)	90
Bethany Fleming (10)	91
Philip McGarry (10)	91
Catherine Braidwood-Harrington (10)	92
Holly Anne Lyas (9)	92
Eleanor Regan (9)	93
Joseph Swann (10)	93
Ben Murphy (10)	94
Michael Westcott (9)	94
Olivia Jones (10)	95
Cameron Bradley (9)	95
Katie Ann Clarke (9)	96
Megan Hynes (9)	96
David Power (11)	97
Ciaran Quinn (9)	97
Alex Davison (9)	98
Nadia Callister (9)	98

Erin Adderley (9)   99
Bethan Blanchfield (9)   99
Marnie Melia (10)   100
Christopher Williams (9)   100
Georgina Murphy (9)   101
Katie Gillespie (9)   101
Lucy Jones (9)   102
Jasmyn Doherty (11)   102
Ella Mooney (10)   103
Luke Wellens (9)   103
Lewis Kenwright (11)   104
Thomas McWilliam (10)   105
Esther Edwards (9)   106
Niamh Oliveira (9)   106

St Peter's Catholic Primary School, Stalybridge
Patrick Hartney (10)   107
Matt O'Brien (10)   107
Cara Headdock (11)   108
Sam Nero (11)   109
Sharon Lunga (10)   110
Cloé Whitehead (10)   110
Joe McDonald (10)   111
Robert McCarthy (10)   111
Kayleigh McGann (10)   112
Holly Sweeney (10)   112
Lucy Sandilands (10)   113
Charlotte Lees (10)   113
Ryan Donlan (10)   114

Sir John Offley CE (VC) Primary School, Madeley
Jordan Halliday (10)   114
Matthew Howard (10)   115
James Stuart (11)   115
Emilee Ward (10)   116
Ryan Jennings (11)   116
Rebecca Kavanagh (10)   117
Emily Parkin (10)   117
James Ball (10)   118
Kyle Dixon (11)   118
Aaron Sumnall (10)   118

The Poems

Shadow

Scornful horror chiselled on your grave,
This will create the beast you crave,
Boneless creature rise from the dead,
With Sir Nicolas' chopped off head.

Decant some infected blood,
Give it eyes that can spy so high,
Whilst dreadful darkness slowly arrives.

Scornful horror chiselled on your grave,
This will create the beast you crave,
Boneless creature rise from the dead,
With Sir Nicolas' chopped off head.

Drop in the scorpion tail,
Shivering and shaking,
Your beast is in the middle of making.

Scornful horror chiselled on your grave,
This will create the beast you crave,
Boneless creature rise from the dead,
With Sir Nicolas' chopped off head.

Wings of a black falcon,
Horns from a devil,
Terror is lurking around,
So make sure you keep your feet glued to the ground.

Scornful horror chiselled on your grave,
This will create the beast you crave,
Boneless creature rise from the dead,
With Sir Nicolas' chopped off head.

Leave a puma clawless,
And make the cauldron floorless,
Grow tall and black,
Never look back.

Emma Cowley & Laura Malam (10)
Beechwood Primary School, Runcorn

Ten Things Found In A Popstar's Handbag

A three foot lipstick,
A five year old CD,
A mirror from ASDA,
A ripped dress from 1972,
A brush made from spiders' webs,
A hat made from apples and glue,
A set of keys to a swimming pool,
Credit card for £1,000,
A pink phone,
A gold microphone.

Rachel Marshall (8)
Beechwood Primary School, Runcorn

My Dog Sash

Sash has always been there since I was a baby girl,
Lying and listening at the side of my cot,
I always remember seeing her.

White soft fur and big brown eyes,
Full of love, now old and wise.

I love my dog Sash right up to the sky,
But she can smell like a pigsty.

Alice Thompson (8)
Beechwood Primary School, Runcorn

The Haunted House

A spooky picture with moving eyes,
A scary ghost with its haunted cries,
A creaky floor as you walk through the door,
Spiders' webs just like lace that stick to your face,
A spooky cat and a witch with a hat,
All these and more behind the big door.

Iona Dunnet (8)
Beechwood Primary School, Runcorn

The Best Of Darkness

Revenge is a dish best served cold,
Blood from my victims,
I'll create a beast so mighty and bold!

Paw of a flabberbat,
Tears from an immortal phoenix,
Then drop in the tail of a dragon, fat.

Revenge is a dish best served cold,
Blood from my victims,
I'll create a beast so mighty and bold!

Add some armour from a malicious knight,
Sprinkle some death and doom,
What a horrible sight!

Revenge is a dish best served cold,
Blood from my victims,
I'll create a beast so mighty and bold!

Throw in some severed bones,
Pour some evil assassination's blood
Then mash in some sharp cones.

Revenge is a dish best served cold,
Blood from my victims,
I'll create a beast so mighty and bold!

Next splash in tendons and muscle,
With the strength of a potent warrior,
Although it might be hard to ignore the bustle.

Revenge is a dish best served cold,
Blood from my victims,
I'll create a beast so mighty and bold!

Grind the foot of a human up,
Then blend it with the silent slithering of a snake,
Leave to set in a giant cup.

Revenge is a dish best served cold,
Blood from my victims,
I'll create a beast so mighty and bold!

Elise Potter (10)
Beechwood Primary School, Runcorn

Chrome The Chaos God

Greedy ravens fly above eating the remains that taste so good,
From my victims whom I stole their blood,
If I were you, I would run if only I could steal your blood!
Add the horror that is chiselled on your grave,
To the wings of a fire bat deep within a fire cave,
That will allow my beast to mingle and mould with thou brave soul,
Greedy ravens fly above eating the remains that taste so good,
From my victims whom I stole their blood,
If I were you I would run if only I could steal your blood!

Melt all those dead bodies down to a bloody gruel
So it can have its fuel,
No one else will be defiant to my crude,
Yet cunning obnoxious giant.

With the might of his allies at his side, all heroes will run and cry,
Greedy ravens fly above eating the remains that taste so good,
From my victims whom I stole their blood,
If I were you, I would run if only I could steal your blood!

Desert woodland marsh our water this beast will hunt down those
Entire little nuisance little brave men for it will never hesitate
Not even for a saint.

Wearing the armour forged in the desert wasteland bearing ancient
Symbols of the dead for this monstrosity will slay all in its path
Greedy ravens fly above eating the remains that taste so good,
From my victims whom I stole their blood,
If I were you I would run if only I could steal your blood
For this is the chaos god Chrome!

Charlie Lecossois (10)
Beechwood Primary School, Runcorn

Treacherous Armoured Trolls

Trolls in metal armour belch,
Ogres in the woods that squelch,
Wolves are howling to the moon,
Create *your* beast of death and doom . . .

Add some turquoise dragon wings,
With some armour from the kings,
Add some bat for radar sense,
With some muscle, nice and tense.

Trolls in metal armour belch,
Ogres in the woods that squelch,
Wolves are howling to the moon,
Create *your* beast of death and doom . . .

Zap some horns in here and there,
Add the teeth from a grizzly bear,
Put a cannon on the back,
So he can fire at his enemy's shack.

Trolls in metal armour belch,
Ogres in the woods that squelch,
Wolves are howling to the moon,
Create *your* beast of death and doom . . .

Put four yellow eyes and two light blue legs,
Decant in some scales and make it lay eggs,
Plonk in some lava breath fire,
Whip in some diamonds from a lady's desire.

Trolls in metal armour belch,
Ogres in the woods that squelch,
Wolves are howling to the moon,
Create *your* beast of death and doom . . .

Mix and churn and mix some more,
You've made your creature,
Now let it explore.

Jonathan Ashton (10)
Beechwood Primary School, Runcorn

Ning, Nang, Nong

(Inspired by 'On the Ning, Nang, Nong' by Spike Milligan)

Ning, nang, nong where the gorilla goes bong,
With a kick from a donkey,
And a smash from a pot,
A shout, shout, shout and
The noise all ends at night,
When the sun comes up,
The bird shouts croak,
You know the noise will be back,
Again in the jungle,
It sounds like jibba jabba ju.

Cameron Barnett (8)
Beechwood Primary School, Runcorn

Glue

Glue on the walls,
Glue on the grass,
Glue on my friend's brass,
Glue on the chair,
Glue everywhere,
In the tub there's none there!

Emily Willis (10)
Betley CE (VC) Primary School, Betley

People Poem

People in the street,
People in the park,
People walking in the town,
People walking in the dark,
People playing with their games,
People playing with their friend Mark,
There's people everywhere except,
In the bathroom because I'm already there.

Connor Bradley Grimes (10)
Betley CE (VC) Primary School, Betley

The Sun And The Wind

The day began,
The sun and the wind,
Were arguing about who was best.
The sun said he was the best,
Of the rest,
But the wind disagreed,
He thought he was best dressed,
The cockerel overheard them,
He said they should have a contest.

The bet, the bet, the sun and wind's bet,
The cockerel said,
'Get that vest off that man's chest,
And you will be best.'
The bet, the bet, the sun and wind's bet,
The wind has a puff,
The man holds on tight,
You haven't done it,
The bet, the bet, the sun and wind's best,
Then the sun had a go,
He heats up the man, he takes off his vest,
'You win!' The cockerel said,
So the wind ran off.

Robert Bellamy (10)
Betley CE (VC) Primary School, Betley

Books Everywhere

Books on the chair,
Books on my hair,
Books in the pool,
Books on the stool,
Books in the tool box,
Books on the floor,
Books everywhere,
Except on the shelf,
No books there.

Olivia Oulton (9)
Betley CE (VC) Primary School, Betley

The Three Pigs

The pigs were too fat to stay in their flat,
So the pig's mother told them to make a new flat.

The flat, the flat, the wonderful flat.

The oldest, Henry, made a flat of straw,
He needed more for the floor.

The flat, the flat, the wonderful flat.

The second oldest, Homer, made a flat of stick,
I think he needed a great big tick.

The flat, the flats, the wonderful flats.

The teeny, weenie little pig, Harry made a flat of bricks,
Now that pig isn't thick.

The flats, the flats, the wonderful flats.

The wolf came and knocked on Henry's door,
I'm blowing your flat down, no need for more chatting,
He blew the flat down with a great big roar!

Poor Homer at the door, the wolf opened into the core.

Harry was proud of his flat,
But what about the wolf's mouth?

The wolf tried and tried to blow down Harry's flat,
But before he could, Harry had cooked him
With his vegetables for tea.

Josh Dutton (10)
Betley CE (VC) Primary School, Betley

Wacky Dancers

(Inspired by 'Ten Happy Schoolboys' by A A Milne)

Ten wacky dancers standing in a line,
One got the giggles and then there were nine.

Nine wacky dangers making a mistake,
One got sacked and then there were eight.

Eight wacky dancers, day dreaming in Heaven,
One got sky sick and then there was seven.

Seven wacky dancers playing with sticks,
One got hypnotised and then there were six.

Six wacky dancers pretending to drive,
One got caught by the policeman and then there were five.

Five wacky dancers skipping out the door,
One had a deadly call and then there were four.

Four wacky dancers climbing a tree,
One couldn't get down and then there were three.

Three wacky dancers on the loo,
One fell in and then there were two.

Two wacky dancers having lots of fun,
One fell asleep and then there was one.

One wacky dancer gained a ton,
She couldn't stand up and then there were none.

Kitty Dolan (10)
Betley CE (VC) Primary School, Betley

People Doing Bad Things
(Inspired by 'Ten Happy Schoolboys' By A A Milne)

Ten bad people doing a crime,
One got caught then there were nine,
Nine bad people vandalising a gate,
One broke his elbow then there were eight,
Eight bad people were in Devon,
One tripped up then there were seven,
Seven bad people wanted a Twix,
The shop owner said get out then there were six,
Six bad people trying to stay alive,
One got shot then there were five,
Five bad people but one was poor,
One got chucked out then there were four,
Four bad people needed a wee,
One went to the toilet then there were three,
Three bad people were in the queue,
One got stuck and then there were two,
Two bad people watching a swan,
One sunk in the lake then there was one,
One bad person gave up and had fun,
There was none left in the group so then there were none.

Daniel Milburn (10)
Betley CE (VC) Primary School, Betley

Ink Poem

Ink on my chair,
Ink in my hair,
Ink on the sofa,
Ink in my bath,
Ink on the mayor,
Ink on a bear,
Ink is everywhere, except
At my nan's, there's no ink
There.

Bradley Hinbest (10)
Betley CE (VC) Primary School, Betley

The Three Little Pigs

Come on you fat pigs,
You're just too big,
There's not enough straw to feed you anymore.

So you're out, you're out, you're out too.

You're just too posh, there's not enough dosh.

Wolfie, Wolfie's really smart, it's just a shame he's got no heart.

The first little pig, of straw made his house,
It's just a shame it couldn't keep out a mouse.

Wolfie, Wolfie's really smart, it's just a shame he has no heart.

The second pig made his house of sticks,
But he's so stupid, he traded it for a Twix.

Wolfie, Wolfie's really smart, it's just a shame he has no heart.

The third pig made his house of bricks,
Left poor old Wolfie in a fix.

The wolf huffed and puffed and chuffed,
'I want to start eating chickens.'

Wolfie, Wolfie's really smart, it's just a shame he has no heart.

Emmie Brookes (9)
Betley CE (VC) Primary School, Betley

Leaves Everywhere

Leaves in the tree,
Leaves on the floor,
Leaves full of bees,
Leaves freezing on the door,
Leaves blowing in the breeze,
Leaves on the shore,
Mr Bold blowing on
The leaves on the yard.

Stephen Burke (9)
Betley CE (VC) Primary School, Betley

The Crow And The Fox

The crow was pleased
When we saw that lovely
Slice of cheese.

The crow, the crow, that silly
Old crow.

He had a peek, picked it
Up with his . . . beak.

The crow, the crow, that silly
Old crow.

Crow saw a tree
Went down, it was free.

The crow, the crow, that silly
Old crow.

Then the fox sniffed him out,
Of that there's no doubt.

The crow, the crow, that silly
Old crow.

The word is you're a
Beautiful bird.

The crow, the crow, that silly
Old crow.

Your voice is the best,
So can I hear?

The crow, the crow, that silly
Old crow.

Crow opened his mouth
Pointed it south,
The cheese fell out onto the fox's snout.

Greg Brookes (9)
Betley CE (VC) Primary School, Betley

The Three Billy Goats Gruff

For the three Billy Goats Gruff,
It's kind of tough,
They've no more grass,
Over the bridge they must pass.

Troll, troll,
You have no soul.

Baby goat is small,
But tough,
For the troll,
He's not enough.

Troll, troll,
You have no soul.

Mummy goat is even tougher,
But she's not big enough to suffer,
Mummy goat was allowed to pass,
To get to the lovely green grass.

Troll, troll,
You have no soul.

Daddy goat was big enough,
He wasn't scared to fight because he was tough,
So Daddy goat began to fight,
With all his might, he hit and pushed,
Kicked the troll for the troll had no soul.

Troll, troll,
You have no soul.

Stephanie Evans (9)
Betley CE (VC) Primary School, Betley

The Hare And The Tortoise

The tortoise
Was going slow and steady,
The hare was going
Fast and ready.

Hare took a nap
Because
Tortoise was
A slow old chap.

The hare was tired out,
But tortoise
Was still about.

He passed the
Winning post
To a gigantic shout . . .

Sebi Herbert-Jackson (10)
Betley CE (VC) Primary School, Betley

In The Air Of The Night

Night is as kind as a cloud in the sky,
He is as soft as a comfortable pillow,
Night is as safe as a prison with guards outside.

He makes you dream sweet dreams,
He is as gentle as a feather,
Floating to the floor,
He has a smooth, black face,
Disguised in the darkness.

His eyes are like stars twinkling, always.

He runs slowly back to his house in a dark alleyway.

Daniel Byrne (10)
Christ the King Catholic Primary School, Wavertree

Night

Night is kind, caring and helpful,
It wanders the lonely valleys looking for a friend,
I am his friend and I am proud of it,
We sometimes fight but that is what friends do.

My friend is very competitive and he hates to lose,
Most of all he takes competition with the sun very seriously
And he tries to win the boys and girls over,
He is well dressed with a golden turban and a ruby waistcoat,
Gold shoes and purple pants.

He is kind just like a grandfather and he picks me up,
Dusts me down so I can continue with whatever it was I was doing.

I go out at night-time to play with Night
Because he's fun to play with,
He is fun to play with.

He always makes me think of sweet dreams,
He is great and I'm glad he's my mate.

Joe O'Neill (10)
Christ the King Catholic Primary School, Wavertree

Night

Night is kind and gentle,
He is very comforting when you are sad,
Night makes you feel safe and secure,
When you are in bed,
He makes you dream sweet dreams
Or even sometimes nightmares,
He dresses all in black, so he can't be seen,
He's not always nice, he can be like a
Silent burglar sometimes,
He moves so quietly he can't be heard.

He can be nice but,
Sometimes bad.

Alex Taylor (11)
Christ the King Catholic Primary School, Wavertree

Night

To me, night is a grinning girl active and running
About mysteriously, her hair is like a soft haystack,
Which she gives to the animals food for them and their family.

She wears clothes which are young and stylish,
And she smells like a fragrant flower,
From a summer's morning.

She moves slowly and dreamily, like walking on the clouds
And she is very good friends with the sun and the moon.

She speaks slowly and quietly, and doesn't wake you up
When she walks around
She lives in the middle of nowhere,
Where no one can find her.
She feels like a duvet washed in washing powder.
Her eyes are like light bulbs,
And twinkling stars in the dark, black sky.

Emma Jones (10)
Christ the King Catholic Primary School, Wavertree

Night

Mrs Midnight comes out to play,
In her pink pyjamas she is,
She glides across the fluffy ground extremely quietly.

Mrs Midnight the village people call,
Please make us fall asleep,
Mrs Midnight sends out her vibes,
And they fall into a delicate comforting sleep.

As she glides, her hair flies carefully with her,
Her lips are a glossy pink,
After she's done her job she glides back to her
Cosy, comfortable house.

Mrs Midnight comes out to play,
In her pink pyjamas she is,
She glides across the fluffy ground extremely quietly.

Rebecca Penketh (10)
Christ the King Catholic Primary School, Wavertree

As The Clock Strikes Night

Night is a pretty young woman,
But don't let that fool you,
She is an evil, dark, red-eyed witch.

Don't make her angry, if you do
She will give you nightmares.

Night is a fast running burglar,
She burgles your sweet dreams away!

Her laugh is so sweet!
Strange for a nasty person isn't it,
It's a lure to catch you in her trap!

Her mouth is an upside down crescent moon,
Her eyes are deep, bloody red fireballs,
Her clothes are silver and they shine in the moonlight.

Night is a pretty young woman,
But don't let that fool you,
She is an evil, dark, red-eyed witch!

Paige O'Neill (10)
Christ the King Catholic Primary School, Wavertree

Night

Night is a cuddly grandma as comforting as can be,
She is a kind and gentle person in every way,
She is a lovely person and lives in a lovely cottage,
Night is a dreamy person,
She is friendly and always happy,
She walks poshly and when she does,
She sounds like a horse wearing horseshoes,
She has hair made from shooting stars,
Her clothes are torn,
She moves swiftly sometimes,
Night can do anything she wants,
A cuddly grandma as comforting as can be.

Katie Craig (10)
Christ the King Catholic Primary School, Wavertree

The Comfort Of The Night

Night is comforting, like a big cuddly teddy bear giving you a hug,
It is kind, just like a grandma reading bedtime stories!
Night is safe,
She is like a security guard, guarding the monstrous
Nightmares from your thoughts,
She tries her best to make you think of sweet,
Soft and gentle dreams,
Night is an old grandma, giving you a great big hug before bed,
When you snuggle down in your duvet, Night will whisper
Muffled calls to you,
She lets you share your problems with her,
She has an old, caring, gentle face, with shining,
Twinkling, starry eyes that sparkle in the crow-black sky,
Night lives in the valley, in a small cottage,
She has a happy, smiling, crescent moon mouth
That calms you down,
She has short, grey, curly locks, that move like a free bird,
Night is the most comforting thing to me!

Megan Doherty (10)
Christ the King Catholic Primary School, Wavertree

Half-Past Night

To me Night is a kind girl running about actively,
Her hair is beautiful golden flocks shining like the sun,
Her clothes are sensible silky robes ready to go to bed,
She moves quickly and swiftly through the mountains,
She speaks quietly so she doesn't wake you up,
She lives in the middle of the mountains near a valley,
Her voice is a deer speaking only kindness,
She feels like a comfortable blanket with special materials,
She smells like fresh air on summer days,
Eyes are twinkling stars on Valentine's Day.

Rachel Bristow (10)
Christ the King Catholic Primary School, Wavertree

Night

Night is calm and gentle,
She's like a loving mum,
She makes you think of sweet dreams,
Of silvery stars in the black velvet sky.

Night's eyes are as bright as stars,
Her mouth speaks soothing and quiet,
Night's hair is black and flowing,
It flows like a river of dreams.

She wears a long black cloak,
It is dark like the midnight sky,
She smells like fragrant flowers,
She feels like a bed of feathers.

Night moves slowly as she plays tricks in shadows,
She lives on top of foggy mountains,
Outside of her mist coloured house,
She flies through the sky like a silent owl.

Hannah Green (10)
Christ the King Catholic Primary School, Wavertree

Sweet Dreams

I meet her every night in my dreams,
Walking down a path in the middle of a valley,
Smiling like a twinkling moonbeam,
Tiptoeing up to the side of your bed,
Whispering dreams into your head,
Her soft wispy hair tickling the side of your cheek,
As she quickly moves back to her cottage on
Top of a mountain peak,
Hiding in her bed as the sun comes up,
She is waiting for another night,
So goodnight sweet dreams.

Beth Newstead (10)
Christ the King Catholic Primary School, Wavertree

Night

Night is a dark mysterious thing,
He sneaks around your house,
When you're alone, he will steal your soul,
He is a burglar taking toys, girls and boys.

He wears a dark, long black cloak,
He hides your toys in there,
He creeps around your house like a teacher
Scraping her long nails on a chalkboard.

If you go to attack Night, even the slightest touch
And he will call out his army and take your soul harder than ever.

Night smells like dead bodies, I am not surprised.

If you try to get on Night's side with a kiss,
It's impossible,
His lips are like the sun.

In winter he is colder than ever,
He will try to get your hair and beard,
I don't like . . . Night!

Christopher Tweedle (10)
Christ the King Catholic Primary School, Wavertree

Night

The night is as big as an iceberg,
He wears dark and bulky clothes,
They make him look fat,
He doesn't like anyone except himself,
He is a sneaky cunning burglar,
He takes toys from boys and girls.

He wears no shoes because he will get heard,
He is as quick as a cheetah,
He is also as scary as a bomb dropping,
His eyes are a terrifying red colour,
He smells like dead bodies.

Daniel Burnett (10)
Christ the King Catholic Primary School, Wavertree

Night

Night is a thief stealing away the sun to cast darkness over us,
He makes me feel unsafe like evil, he lurks in every corner,
His face is shadowy and dark like a million nightmares,
Trapped in every shadow,
His eyes dark as coal never to be burnt into ashes,
Those black lips that never speak kind, good or caring words
Cover fangs as big as fish with a tongue of a snake,
More poisonous than anything on Earth,
His hair, greasy and black falls down to his broad shoulders,
His clothes are black gowns made of bad dreams,
That covers his bare black feet which hover over the Earth,
He speaks in his low voice, sown into him with a thousand
Children's screams, he strikes you with terror,
He lives in a dark, damp cave with no one and hides away
When the sun comes back looking for him,
Night hates me and I hate Night.

Lauren Taylor (10)
Christ the King Catholic Primary School, Wavertree

Night

Night is a kind and caring person who loves you,
He makes you comforting, safe and happy,
It makes you feel like you're not on your own,
You have sweet dreams like a caring grandpa,
Keeping you cosy and warm.

It has bright yellow trousers with a green top,
His skin shining like a horse glancing through a field,
His teeth shining like a ghost looking into the iceberg,
His hair blowing through the wind.

He lives in the long caves in the tall mountains,
With no shoes, tiptoeing quietly and slow,
Night gives you happy thoughts when you're safe,
Night gives you the biggest smile every day.

Shaun Stafford (10)
Christ the King Catholic Primary School, Wavertree

Night

Mr Night is comforting and as kind as a grandpa,
He comforts you and makes you cosy and warm,
He makes you feel safe and have dreams that are sweet.

Mr Night helps you have sweet and kind dreams,
Full of happiness and joy,
Mr Night is as caring as a grandma hugging you.

Mr Night helps you imagine kind things at night,
His face as soft and gentle as a pillow,
His eyes crystal blue full of joy and envy,
His mouth as gentle, quiet and soft as velvet.

His hair as smooth and gentle as dog's fur,
His spooky black cloak as smooth as silk,
He moves very gentle, slowly and calm,
He lives in a lovely soft field of wheat
That is comfy and cosy,
Mr Night helps you get to sleep
And dream of wonderful things.

Alex Walmsley (10)
Christ the King Catholic Primary School, Wavertree

Night

Night is a burglar,
He makes me feel scared and frightened,
His face has a smile,
His eyes are dull and very dark,
His hair is long and black,
He wears a big heavy coat, black T-shirt and blue jeans,
His mouth is as wide as an elephant,
Night moves quickly and stomps loudly,
When he speaks his voice is dark and loud,
He lives in a flat with his American pitbull,
The flat has broken windows.

Thomas Feeley (10)
Christ the King Catholic Primary School, Wavertree

Night

Night is like a caring, sharing grandma,
She makes me feel safe and comforted,
Night's face is soft, caring and smooth,
Her eyes are like blocks of gold shining in the sky,
Her lips are as red as rubies,
Her hair is as smooth as the finest silk sheet
And as dark as the darkest brown,
Her clothes are made of silk and are as light as snow,
When she moves the whole world relaxes with nothing to think of,
When night speaks, she makes a field of flowers sway in the breeze,
Night likes to be as kind as summer days and
As evil as winter nights,
Night lives in a three-storey house with dawn and
The roof is covered with a thin layer of snow,
Night is fantastic, it makes me feel happy and dreamful.

Lauren Heames (10)
Christ the King Catholic Primary School, Wavertree

Night

Night is nasty,
He is scary,
He makes me feel lonely inside,
He makes me scared and gives me nightmares,
He is a burglar creeping silently in the house,
When it goes dark, he breaks in!
He is very scary!
His eyes are red,
His mouth is red as blood,
His hair is black as coal,
Night moves with the moon,
He lives anywhere but my house,
Night scares!

Jennifer Ruglen (10)
Christ the King Catholic Primary School, Wavertree

Night

In the night Mrs Moonlight comes out to do her job,
She wears her silken divine duvet pyjamas,
Every night she glides beside each house.

Mrs Moonlight clicks her fingers over every chimney,
She waits for her magic to begin, she looks in the window
And sees people fall asleep.

As the sun rises, Mrs Moonlight does too,
She floats back up to her home,
Mrs Moonlight goes back to the moon.

In the night, Mrs Moonlight comes out to do her job,
She wears her silken divine duvet pyjamas,
Every night she glides beside each house.

Megan Jones (10)
Christ the King Catholic Primary School, Wavertree

Night

Night is very wonderful,
Night is comfortable and caring,
Night is very safe and kind,
Night makes me have nice dreams,
Night is a caring granpa cuddling me,
Night looks after me,
Night has a sparkling face,
Night has stars as eyes,
Night has a moon for a mouth,
Night has hair full of stars,
Night has clothes like Jesus,
Night moves slowly and gently,
Night lives over my house,
Night tucks me in at night.

Benjamin McNally (10)
Christ the King Catholic Primary School, Wavertree

Moonlight Night

I got a note from the Princess of Moonlight,
Her golden hair of velvet silk and twinkling face,
She sits and daydreams at a diamond creek,
Snug tight,
In a silent and spacey place.

Her long sleeved nightgown of silver gems and white,
A voice so pure it makes me sleep of the sweetest dreams,
Her eyes of midnight black and a pupil of white for her sight,
A fragrance of a midnight rose meadow so it seems.

Silent toes of feathers, slippers not worn,
She lives in a house of misty stardust,
Moves like a flowing dream, a promise never torn,
Moon butterflies fluttering in a silent dust.

Rachel Pearce (11)
Christ the King Catholic Primary School, Wavertree

Night

Night is kind and comforting,
Night is scary but very kind,
Nothing is happening in the pitch-black dark,
He lives in a house in the valley tops.

Mr Night is lonely, a burglar too,
Taking children's toys, keeping them,
Under his big black cloak,
Sneaking like a cat scratching his back.

His face is happy but strange,
Flames around his eyes, spiky blonde hair,
Very slowly,
Watch out, he will scare you.

Jonathan Turner (10)
Christ the King Catholic Primary School, Wavertree

Night

Night is a comfortable thing like a warm fire,
Night is loving and caring to you like a family member,
Night is my best mate, he's great,
When I am alone, he protects me.

He doesn't give me nightmares,
He gives me sweet dreams of sweet things,
He is peaceful, he is warm, he is cool and he hates school,
He is peaceful, he is great,
He would never steal from me.

He smells like a newborn baby that just came out of the hospital,
He camouflages in the moon, never mind he is the moon,
In winter he tries not to keep me cold,
He's always smiling even when someone lets him down,
He lives in the sky, he only comes out when it's dark,
He doesn't have a normal-shaped head,
He has a moon-shaped head,
I'm asleep for hours so he must move slowly,
Night is better than light,
He doesn't wear any shoes to keep me asleep,
He lives on Mount Everest ready to come down,
He has red hot lips and one of the best voices in the whole world.

Jonny Dwyer (10)
Christ the King Catholic Primary School, Wavertree

Night

Night is a kind, caring grandpa who gives you sweets,
He makes me feel soft and comfortable,
He is as nice as chocolate and as cool as a freezer,
He is brilliant,
He becomes relaxed and as calm as a tree,
He is like a cat so silent and so sweet,
He is my night!

Thomas Sergeant (10)
Christ the King Catholic Primary School, Wavertree

Night

Night is a loving, caring grandpa,
He makes me feel safe, not scared and comforted,
His face looks like a nice star,
His eyes are like ice blue water,
His mouth is like a juicy round apple,
His hair is dark brown like a tree,
His clothes are made like cuddly pyjamas,
When he moves, he has light feet like stars,
When he speaks he has good manners,
He lives on a diamond with a cuddly teddy floating in the sky.

Morgan Smith (10)
Christ the King Catholic Primary School, Wavertree

Night

Night is a very scary, nasty place like a horrible storm,
Night is very scary - in the dark,
Night, it's a lonely place,
Night can give you nightmares,
Night is a burglar creeping into my house,
Night has a dark blue face like an Everton kit,
Night's hair is very, very big, like a great white shark,
Night's clothes are very light blue,
Night lives in the dark forest,
Night will haunt you!

Daniel Fenech (10)
Christ the King Catholic Primary School, Wavertree

Night

Night is a caring granpa who makes me feel safe,
He has a circular mouth,
He wears a black suit and has black hair and blue eyes,
He moves like a butterfly and speaks like a dog,
He lives in space with his family.

Patrick Jolliffe (10)
Christ the King Catholic Primary School, Wavertree

Night

Night is a nasty man and he makes me scared and lonely,
He makes me have nightmares,
It's face looks like a chocolate muffin,
His eyes are like raisins and his mouth is like a round orange,
The night whistles as you walk down the lane,
His hair is like brown chocolate milkshake,
Swishing around the cup as you drink it,
His clothes are ragged like old pieces of cloth ripped and torn,
When he moves, he moves like a quiet mouse asleep in its bed,
He screams like a one-year-old baby when he's angry and scared,
He lives in a cloud.

Sean Dignum (10)
Christ the King Catholic Primary School, Wavertree

Night

Night is a kind and caring man, who makes me feel safe,
He makes me feel comforting and he always keeps his eye on me,
Night makes me have sweet dreams of care,
He is a sweet and caring grandpa,
Night makes me think about him,
Night has a very mushy face,
His eyes are deep brown like a tree trunk,
His mouth is large, his hair is as black as the sky,
Night's clothes are very clean,
Night sways through the sky, he lives on a very special cloud,
He always cares about me.

Jack Wright (11)
Christ the King Catholic Primary School, Wavertree

Night

Night is a nurse, calm and always there to help,
She makes me feel calm with her soothing voice,
Her face has a daydreaming expression,
Her eyes shine and sparkle like stars,
Her lips are dark, shaded and grey,
Her hair is jet-black and straight,
Her long flowing silky white clothes are illuminated in the dark,
When she moves she takes long, slow, wide paces,
When she speaks, she takes deep breaths
And her soothing voice makes you feel drowsy,
She lives in a castle in the country by herself,
She calms me down.

Jamie Pye (10)
Christ the King Catholic Primary School, Wavertree

Night

Night is a comforting time of day,
She makes me feel sleepy,
Her face is a resting place,
Her eyes are droopy,
Her mouth is still and closed,
Her hair is down, long and dark,
Her clothes are loungy,
She moves slowly, floating across the sky,
When she speaks, it makes me sleepy,
She lives high up in the sky with her mum and dad,
Night warms me.

Olivia Symes (11)
Christ the King Catholic Primary School, Wavertree

Night-A-Lishes

Night is kind, comforting, safe and is caring like a grandpa,
Night is cool, cooler than school he is great, he's my best mate,
Night hates to lose, he's got no shoes,
Night is kind, comforting, safe and is caring like a grandpa.

Night takes coins off girls and boys, gives them back better than toys,
Night loves to rest, he eats eggs out off a nest,
Night takes coins off girls and boys, gives them back better than toys.

Night is bright, brighter than light,
Night lets you sleep all through the week,
Night lives in a warm and cosy house and has a big fat mouse,
Night is bright, brighter than light.

Joe Jones (10)
Christ the King Catholic Primary School, Wavertree

Night

Night is a kind and caring grandma,
She makes me feel comforted,
Her face is made out of shining stars,
Her eyes are dark and green,
She has got a starry smile,
Her hair is blond,
Her clothes are shimmering,
She skips when she moves,
She speaks calmly and softly,
She lives in a cottage made of stars,
She lulls me to sleep.

Rebecca O'Gorman (10)
Christ the King Catholic Primary School, Wavertree

Night

Night is a caring mother,
She makes me feel safe and happy,
Her eyes are like stars,
Her face is as bright as the moon,
Her mouth is like a shooting star,
Her hair is long and golden,
Her clothes are long and black,
She walks barefooted through the sky,
She speaks like a bird tweeting,
She lives in the sky with the man in the moon,
The night is a good friend.

Daniel Owens (10)
Christ the King Catholic Primary School, Wavertree

Night

Night is a caring, loving grandma,
She makes me feel happy,
Her face looks like sweet petals,
Her eyes are dark blue,
Her smile is full of stars,
Her hair is thick and long,
She usually wears dark blue or black,
She moves like the wind,
When she speaks, it's as light as a feather,
Night makes me feel happy.

Katie O'Malley (10)
Christ the King Catholic Primary School, Wavertree

When Piggy Went

When Piggy went,
I had nothing,
No little face,
Peeking out,
From my pencil case,
No little face,
To keep me company,
Whilst doing my homework.

Those first few nights,
I cried myself to sleep,
Until I got Piggy 2,
Fatter than Piggy,
But with the same face and smile.

During those ten months,
I hoped,
I prayed,
For Piggy,
Wherever he was.

Then came,
September,
When Piggy was discovered,
In the book box.

Victoria Relf (10)
Crowton Christ Church CE Primary School, Northwich

The Gim Gam Goodle

(Inspired by 'On the Ning Nang Nong' by Spike Milligan)

The gim gam goodle,
Has a pet Wang doodle,
And jumps from tree to tree,
Tomorrow we're going on a picnic,
I hope he doesn't see me.

The gim gam goodle,
Eats mish and Kaboodle,
And picks out all the bones,
On Saturdays he goes for walks,
And crunches on pine cones.

The gim gam goodle,
Harvests noodles by the
Light of the moon,
And uses sheep and goats,
To bring them to your spoon.

So the gim gam goodle,
May be good and may be bad,
But for all we know,
He's the weirdest creature,
This world's ever had,
Or is he?

Imani Caine (10)
Crowton Christ Church CE Primary School, Northwich

Deep Water Riddle

Drying in the sun,
Sprawled across the sand,
Round and round my body curves,
One of the slimiest things on land.

I once drifted in a place so deep,
There were only slits of light,
With swimming creatures bold as brass,
It was a nightmare of the night.

Soon I will return to that,
I mutter with a sigh,
But before I do, may I ask.
What am I?

(Seaweed.)

Kara McCarthy (10)
Crowton Christ Church CE Primary School, Northwich

Summer On The Beach In Cornwall!

Dazzling blue sea,
Seagulls flying in and out,
White waves are curling!

Sunrays are bouncing,
The happiness is catching,
Shells are all around!

Running through the sand,
It's the height of surfing time,
My Cornish summer!

Rebecca Annells (10)
Crowton Christ Church CE Primary School, Northwich

Young Writers - Little Laureates Poems From The North West

Horses

H orses are fast when they gallop,
O ver the jumps they go,
R iding in bright coloured coats,
S tampeding across the courses,
E nding at the winning post,
S addles off the winning horses.

Claire Campbell (9)
Crowton Christ Church CE Primary School, Northwich

The High Street

I was walking down the high street one sunny day,
I could smell the luscious food,
It was chocolate brown kebabs,
I could hear the blasting exhausts that rushed from cars,
The exhausts were gigantic,
They were rattling like mad,
I touched the brass handle on my door,
I opened the door to my cosy home,
I go to bed and I fall straight to sleep.

Tom Wolstenholme (10)
Dane Bank Primary School, Stockport

Seasons

In springtime I can taste the delicious creamy chocolate
The Easter bunny left behind.
I can smell the white blossom tickling my nose like a feather.
I can hear chicks chirping quietly while their mum feeds them worms.
I can see rabbits jumping in the fields and the frogs in the ponds.
I can hear the footsteps in the white snow.
I can see people skiing down the mountains.
I can taste the glimmering snow in my mouth.

Adam Whiting (8)
Dane Bank Primary School, Stockport

Seasons

In wintertime I glimpse at sparkly snow on the ground.

I hear cars sliding loudly on the road.

I touch the freezing snow,
I smell muddy footprints,
I see my friend darting down the hill.

Summer
I observe the scorching beach,
I hear children shouting loudly,
I feel the sun's warmth on my cheeks,
I smell barbecues cooking, lovely.

In spring
I smell the delicious Easter eggs,
I touch melty Easter eggs,
I smell the juicy flowers,
I see Easter bunnies bouncing.

Aaron James Bray (8)
Dane Bank Primary School, Stockport

Seasons

In wintertime
I can perceive the perishing icy snow being crushed,
I can gather snow crackling like a paper bag being thrown in the bin,
I can nuzzle inflexible solid trees,
I can sense burning wood like a house on fire!

In springtime
I can regard the dainty daisies developing in the sun,
I can discover dogs on walks,
I can manipulate the gorgeous blossom trees,
I can feel the boiling sweet sun shining on me.

Molly Keane (8)
Dane Bank Primary School, Stockport

Seasons

In wintertime
I perceive the uncovered trees that shine,
I listen to the sound of hooting owls,
I fondle freezing snow,
I smell the car's fuel.

In summertime
I witness my presents on the floor,
I listen to the splashes in the paddling pool,
I fondle the cool water,
I smell the smoke of the BBQ rising slowly.

In autumn time
I discern the golden leaves,
I hear rattling trees,
I feel the crunchy leaves,
I smell the aroma of the engine from the lawnmower.

In springtime
I behold the daffodils that look like the sun,
I hear the chickens being noisy,
I dab the concise chicks,
I sniff new life.

Lewis Appleton-Jones (8)
Dane Bank Primary School, Stockport

Seasons

In springtime I can taste delicious creamy,
Chocolate Easter bunny left behind.
I can smell the fragrant daffodils in the Victorian park.
I can hear chicks clamouring in the bushes.
I can touch wildlife in the Tudor park.
In wintertime I can taste the icy snow.
I can see the snowflakes fluttering down.
I can hear robins chirping in the bare trees.
I can smell my hot chocolate boiling up.
I can touch the hot mug heating me.

Cameron Atkinson (9)
Dane Bank Primary School, Stockport

Seasons

In autumn time
I can discover lovely flowers,
I can hear banging of pretty fireworks,
I can feel leaves hitting me like a frozen rabbit,
Fragrance of fire warming people up hits me as I walk by.

In springtime
I can observe baby animals being born,
I can gather birds tweeting in their nests,
I can stroke baby animals that have just been born,
I can smell lovely flowers.

In wintertime
I can regard white crunchy snow like cold toast,
I can hear people playing on sledges,
I can manipulate freezing snowmen,
I can see bare trees like fluffy white clouds.

Megan Zoe Roberts (8)
Dane Bank Primary School, Stockport

Seasons

In wintertime I glimpse huge presents,
I can hear the loud crunch of my big feet in the snow,
I glimpse at the treats when I come in from Hallowe'en,
I can smell the barbecue roasting in the back garden.

In autumn time I glimpse my boiling, steaming hot tea,
I can hear the strong wind brushing through the big, long branches,
I can touch the freezing cold crispy leaves,
I can smell horrible stinking little fish.

In summertime I glimpse the boiling sea,
I can touch the bright golden sand,
I can smell the vast long salty sea.

George Dey (8)
Dane Bank Primary School, Stockport

Seasons

In wintertime I can listen to people merrily laughing
                                        dodging snowballs,
I can touch the very cold, white snow,
I can smell invisible smoke from fireworks,
I can spy the bare trees.

In summer I can stroke the yellow sand from the beach,
I can smell the salty sea,
I can listen to the birds singing up the trees like people
                                        blowing in a recorder.

In autumn I can see the huge trees with green,
                                        yellow and red leaves,
I can smell the smoke coming across my nose,
I can scrape the colourful leaves up in the blue sky,
I can listen to singing up in the trees.

In spring I can see the new small shining flowers,
I can smell the beautiful smelly flowers,
I can feel the leaves on the low trees,
I can hear the shaking trees in the garden.

Zoe Higham (8)
Dane Bank Primary School, Stockport

All About My City Poem

One sunny hot morning I was going to the city to do some shopping,
I saw my friend,
So I chatted to her for five minutes,
Then I walked away to the toy shop,
Because I was buying a present for my best friend Charley,
The shelves were full of toys,
Every shelf was full,
My friend is 7 years old,
So I bought a soft teddy bear,
I went round to her house and gave it to her,
At night she took it to bed and snuggled up in bed with it.

Molly Wolstenholme (7)
Dane Bank Primary School, Stockport

My City Poem

Walking through the city centre,
I noticed I could see lots and lots of lovely looking shops,
That really amused me,
First I went in the games shop,
With digital games to play,
I bought two games that were three pounds each,
Then I came out of the games shop,
I heard some cars skid,
It was because there had been a giant crash!
I was so scared, I rushed away,
After that I smelt some food,
I arrived there, it was burger and chips,
I was so hungry,
I started to eat straight away.

Aaron Dunne (8)
Dane Bank Primary School, Stockport

Seasons

In wintertime,
I can gaze at the white snow,
I can listen to the huge bells,
I can feel the freezing snowballs,
I can observe the people coming,
Down on their sledges like class 4,
Rushing out of the classroom because
The fire alarm goes off.

In springtime,
I can discern the lovely birds,
I can hear the rattling trees,
I can stroke the cuddly rabbits,
I can smell the odour of the roses.

Benjamin Powell (8)
Dane Bank Primary School, Stockport

The City

Walking through the city,
I noticed there was a delicious food stall nearby,
So I tried to fight the smell,
Then I found an enormous café,
It was crowed with customers,
On the pavement there was garbage all over,
I hopped out of the shop,
I went to discover something else,
I was excited,
I might find an arcade shop around the corner,
And there was an arcade shop,
I ran in,
There were loads of cool games,
I didn't know which to try first,
Then I heard an engine outside,
I went out, it was my bus,
I hopped on and it took me home.

Edward Mooney (7)
Dane Bank Primary School, Stockport

My City Poem

I could smell something good,
It smelt like cake, carrot cake,
My favourite, I saw an orange fox
And her cubs at night-time,
Messing in my rubbish bags
And when they went away,
I went to bed,
At daytime, I heard something else,
Some traffic near my flat,
I went to see what was wrong,
It was some road works,
Making a massive traffic jam.

Luann Jordan Dickson (7)
Dane Bank Primary School, Stockport

My City Poem

Walking through the city centre,
I saw the noisy video game shop,
Inside there where new shiny games,
I heard pigeons flapping their wings
And I saw this tree with beautiful blue flashing lights,
I could smell a hot dog stand,
A burger stand and a McDonald's bar,
I feel the darkness all around me,
I can feel the bark on the trees,
I felt the watery wet window inside the shops,
I saw a lot of cars, their engines causing pollution,
I felt the rust on a metal chair,
I saw the birds in the sky
And I saw a rainbow.

Daniel Evans (8)
Dane Bank Primary School, Stockport

The High Street

I was strolling down the high street one rainy day,
And I spotted a smart and kind man,
Helping an old pensioner with very heavy shopping bags.

One sunny day I was dawdling slowly down the road,
I smelt mouth-watering doughnuts,
That tinkled my nose.

I was walking in huge giant steps,
And I touched the door handle,
And it was as cold as an ice pack.

Reece Hampstead (10)
Dane Bank Primary School, Stockport

My City Poem

Walking through the city centre,
I spotted a sports shop,
I went in and I saw the sportiest Nike trainers in the shop,
I bought the sportiest Nike trainers,
Then I smelt the beautiful hot dogs with smoked sausage,
I drooled at the lovely smell,
I bought the smoked sausages,
I heard a massive pigeon soaring through the sky,
It went into its nest,
Then its egg started to wobble,
Then it hatched!
I gasped with my eyes open,
My mouth was as wide as a shark's mouth,
It was the cutest thing I had ever seen!

Cameron Thompson (7)
Dane Bank Primary School, Stockport

The City

I jumped on a bus and visited Stockport,
When I got off the bus,
I saw birds weaving in the sky and
Felt glass windows and I saw my reflection in them,
I could smell McDonald's,
So I followed the smell,
Until I found McDonald's,
But then I could smell garbage,
It smelt horrible,
I heard birds sing a lovely song in the trees
And then I heard an egg crack in the nest
And a baby bird tried to fly
But he fell out of the sky into the city street.

Jack Cope (8)
Dane Bank Primary School, Stockport

My Dance Exam

Putting my hair in a pony tail,
I'll be upset if I fail,
I hope I get my certificate in the mail,
I saw the examiner and she's a female.

My heart is beating fast,
My mum is here to support me,
She is waving in the crowd happily,
If I mess up everyone will see,
It's time to go in at last.

The examiner stares and writes things down,
If I don't do it right, people will frown,
If I win I will feel like royalty wearing a crown,
My grandma is here from another town,
Now I'm ready to start my dances,
The first dance is Britney Spears,
I look at the crowd with all my fears,
If I don't pass I'll be in tears,
In this dance, there are lots of twirls and prances.

The last dance is the hardest of all,
There are lots of jumps so I hope I don't fall,
On the big stage I look really small,
I hear my mum shout and call,
The music stops and I am done,
Everyone claps and says, 'That was great.'
I look around and see Yasmin, she's my best mate,
I'm glad she came even though she was late,
I say to myself, *that was really fun.*

My mum says well done when I get home,
I hear a ring and it's the phone,
My mum says, 'Hello' in a very nice tone,
I shout up to Joe, 'I'm home,' and he starts to moan.
'The examiner wants to speak to you,'
The lady says, 'You didn't fail.
I'll send you your certificate in the mail,'
'Mum, I did it,' I begin to wail,
'I'm so happy I can't believe it's true.'

Hannah Rachael Costin (11)
Dane Bank Primary School, Stockport

The Cruise

I'm going on the cruise today,
All that boring packing I say,
I have no time to mess and play,
The coach is here, it takes all day,
As I am going on a cruise,
Waiting to get on the ship,
As I am going, I bite my lip,
Careful on the gangway, don't trip!
As I am getting closer to the ship.

I show my pass, finally I'm through,
There are so many things to do,
I meet a couple called Mick and Sue,
I make friends, they're fun too,
Finally I'm on the ship,
Now I dance and prance around,
I fall and make a big sound,
As I go and hit the ground,
I am now officially on the ship.

I go and get a nice ice cream,
I meet the captain and his team,
I see a nice singer so I scream,
Then I licked my whipped up cream,
I'm so excited on the ship,
I get my hair and make-up done,
Then I get a photo shoot in the sun,
I just had lots and lots of fun,
On the sun deck of the ship.

Yeah we're setting off at last,
The ship is going really fast,
I'm leaving Manchester in the past,
I'm heading towards a sunny forecast,
It's going to be great on the ship,
I am going for a dip in the pool,
I am so not missing school,
In the swimming pool I look so cool,
It's really great on the ship.

Rebecca Sarah Large (10)
Dane Bank Primary School, Stockport

On My Bike

Me, Sam and Kane have arranged to meet while I'm on my bike.

Building a ramp is really tough,
We collect all kinds of stuff,
Get a splinter, the wood was rough,
Make it just tall enough,
While I'm on my bike,
Our tyres are chewed by Sam's dog,
The weather is changing here comes the fog,
Time to go for some roast hog,
When I play on my bike.

The stunt peg is always stuck,
The black seat is always full of muck,
On my tyre there is poo from a duck,
Every time my mum sees it she says, 'Yuck,'
When I'm getting my bike,
My dad comes out to cut the grass,
It can't hold the grass because of the mass,
Just as I am leaving my mum says, 'There's no gas,'
When I get my blue bike.

Getting away from my dad is hard,
To get to the gate, I need to go a yard,
My brother thinks he is a guard,
Mum says, 'You can't have bacon, there's no lard.'
When I am on my bike,
Unlocking the gate is a tough job,
It is hard because there's no knob,
Just as I'm leaving, my dad's friends comes, he's called Rob,
As I'm going to Sam's on my bike.

You have to wait for them to open the jaw,
When they do, it's not Sam so you have to wait more,
He has to get his shoes off the floor,
Finally he comes through the door,
While I am on my bike,
Sam's mum says, 'Put all the shoes neat,'
While we play on the street.

Michael Cope (10)
Dane Bank Primary School, Stockport

Michael's Football

Mum shouts to me from the bottom stair,
She tells me to brush my hair,
We're in a rush to get there,
But I have no reason to care,
Because it's Michael's football!
Michael and Jack are always ready,
I'm just taking it steady,
I want to go back to bed with my teddy,
And not to Michael's football.

It starts raining when we come,
All my ten toes are numb,
I have a moan to my mum,
And I have an empty tum,
I don't like Michael's football!
Jack has fallen and is in pain,
While we're standing in the rain,
His crying and moaning drives me insane,
I hate Michael's football!

There are no toilets and I need a pee,
There is nothing to occupy me,
I just want a hot cup of tea,
And there's a man in the way so I can't see!
What's going on at Michael's football?
The match always starts late,
And my pee cannot wait,
I really wish I ate,
Before Michael's football.

It's time to go home, hip hip hooray!
I'm going to stay in all day,
I'm not going to go out and play,
On this very rainy day,
We've finished at Michael's football,
I wish I could go to bed,
I have a very dizzy head,
'I'm so glad, I won,' Michael says,
I'm glad we're home from Michael's football.

Danielle Cope (10)
Dane Bank Primary School, Stockport

A Holiday At A Caravan Park

We have to get up early today,
Because we're going on holiday,
I hope we don't get stuck on the way!
Dad says it's fun there, hip, hip, hooray!
We're staying at a caravan park,
After a few hours we finally arrive,
My sister screams, she saw a beehive,
Anne lives near a beach where people dive,
Dad starts shouting so we don't lark.

We park in a space near the beach side,
Grandma tells Abi about the tide,
I spot them all as they try to hide,
I made friends with a boy called Clyde,
We're staying at a caravan park,
We talk about how we've been,
Anne's the size of a middle-age teen,
When Anne talks to people, she's not mean,
Dad's still shouting so we don't lark.

My sister shouts, 'We're here, we're here.'
But Daddy just wants a nice, large beer,
My sister hurts her foot, she wipes a tear,
My mum says get into gear,
We've arrived at the caravan park.

Mum gets a tan from the hot red sun,
While we swim Gran gets us a bun,
I lift my sister, she weighs a tonne,
Dad keeps shouting so we don't lark.

We enjoyed the rest of our time there,
On the way back, everyone would care,
We got stuck in traffic from there,
A lorry crashed, we couldn't bare,
Now we're leaving the caravan park,
I wish we could stay all day,
As we weren't in traffic on the way,
But we're back at home, *hip hip hooray,*
Dad starts snoring - it's turned dark.

Alexandra Faulkner (10)
Dane Bank Primary School, Stockport

The High Street

The high street is a mess and it should be cleaned up,
I could smell something disgusting and I almost threw up my tea,
I walked into the chippy and had some chips,
I had a chip and it was as hard as a pip,
The weather got stormy and the high street started to bore me,
I started to shiver like an ice cube,
My knees started to wobble,
And I saw a girl wearing a bobble,
I saw some boys playing football,
And they kicked the ball and it popped,
It popped on the road like a dot,
I dashed home as fast as I could,
To get in my cosy bed and go to sleep.

Ben Lewis Etchells (9)
Dane Bank Primary School, Stockport

My City Poem

I noticed that birds were flying over my head,
I smelt lovely hot dogs and I wanted one,
I heard cars and motorbikes and I heard their engines,
I could smell garbage on the ground, it smelt horrible,
I noticed people chattering on the city pavement,
I saw dogs and cats, the dogs were chasing the cats,
I walked into the Game shop, I heard the beeping,
I could smell burgers from Burger King and some chips,
I was running really fast and I tripped over a stone,
I saw a shop that sold plasters so then I bought one.

Kyle Moore (7)
Dane Bank Primary School, Stockport

My City Poem

Walking through the city centre,
I looked at a shop called ASDA,
It was ginormous,
I went in and smelt lots of food
And went for food at the Café,
Then I went to an arcade room
And everyone was shouting,
Also I met my friend Jack
And went to the fair.

Stephen Nevins (8)
Dane Bank Primary School, Stockport

Autumn

When I walk through the park I see
Squirrels climbing around the tree,
Ducks bobbing up and down,
Birds twisting and twirling in the sky,
Rabbits burrowing into the earth,
Leaves floating gently down,
Dogs stumbling with their walker.

Jack Breary (10)
Longbarn Community Primary School, Warrington

Autumn Poem

Can you hear the birds tweeting?
Can you hear the ducks quacking?
Yes you can,
No you can't,
Yes you can,
'Cause I hear leaves crackling,
There are birds gliding,
You can see red and orange leaves.

Jake Wall (10)
Longbarn Community Primary School, Warrington

Autumn Senses

I can hear chattering birds,
Flying overhead.

I can see multicoloured leaves,
Scattered on the ground.

I can taste the autumn air,
Hitting the back of my throat.

I can smell a duck pond,
In the distance.

I can feel the smooth leaves,
Floating in my pocket.

Paul Cordingley (11)
Longbarn Community Primary School, Warrington

My Autumn Imagination

I imagine a place,
In the world,
Full of different coloured flowers,
I am there for days,
And hours and hours,
I sit there and gaze,
Under the conker tree,
Then one falls and hits me.

Megan Breary (10)
Longbarn Community Primary School, Warrington

I Can See

I can see ducks, leaves, trees,
Some twigs and a bird,
Autumn leaves on the ground,
Red,
Yellow, green and brown.

Lewis Hanglin (9)
Longbarn Community Primary School, Warrington

I Can See . . .

I can see a pond,
I can see a duck,
I can see a forest full of trees,
I can see a bunch of leaves that have floated to the ground.

I can see a pretty pink flower,
I can see a bush,
I can see people sitting on a bench,
I can see a picnic table,
I can see a train running along the train track,
I can see a park,
I can see a field of grass,
I can see a rabbit,
I can see *autumn*.

Jessica Neild (9)
Longbarn Community Primary School, Warrington

Autumn Is Arriving

Leaves are crunching,
Ducks are quacking,
Nature is running,
Trees are dying,
Autumn is coming,
Animals hibernate,
Leaves are falling,
Rabbits are running,
Autumn is coming!
And . . .
Squirrels are climbing,
Leaves are twisting,
Autumn is arriving.

Sam Vernon (10)
Longbarn Community Primary School, Warrington

Senses

S eventy million ducks in the pond (or so it seems),
E very duck swimming for bread,
N ice different colours like maroon, yellow, amber and scarlet,
S ome trees are bare and their leaves make a carpet rich and rare,
E very colour leaves fluttering and floating like all the others,
S ome are ragged, some have curves, but this leaf is special . . .
Because it's mine.

Charlotte Hulme (10)
Longbarn Community Primary School, Warrington

Autumn

We are the kids of Longbarn School,
I love autumn because it's cool.

Every day in autumn kids have fun,
In the leaves and without the sun.

In the trees, there is a breeze,
Where squirrels throw nuts at our knees.

Green, yellow, red, dead,
Put the leaves in the shed.

Dominic McAlinden (10)
Longbarn Community Primary School, Warrington

Sadness

Sadness is royal blue like a fresh drop of somebody's tears,
Sadness sounds like a baby crying in the darkness of its bed,
It smells like ice frozen in the cold freezer,
It looks like a pool full of melted ice,
It feels like the sea roaring and the waves crashing together,
Sadness reminds me of when I walked into a tree
And a bit of bark went in my eye.

Liam Johnston (8)
Lower Park Primary School, Poynton

My Lowry Poem

The wide windows as great as the world's tallest giraffe,
They were crumbling unsteady bricks as crumbly as a
                              Flake chocolate bar,
Steep slippery steps loom up at the houses steeper
Than Mount Everest,
In the town huge masses of black polluted smoke would
Rise out of the dark houses.

Smokey streets too gloomy for sun,
Drive around if you dare as there are holey pavements
That lock you up like a darting dungeon prison beware!
Gritty roads form atmosphere like the beach
Making young children be hurt!
Single lamp posts stand alone just like the figures,
All sad in the polluted smoggy roads.

The gloomy sky unable to reach the stars
With the thick solid gas that floats above as black as a child's eye,
The feel of the dusty roads,
There were no birds because of the treacherous smoke
And the terrifying hunters,
When you climb up the steps to your house
And scrub your face, the water that was once clear would
Have turned to black, disgraceful polluted gas!

Children with hunched shoulders, the poor souls,
The way they plod, their bones creak every step of the way,
Their disability enables them to only bow their heads in agony.

The stray dogs roam around hobbling frantically unaware
Of the neck strangling pollution,
The black dogs sniffing heavily like a horrendous tornado,
Lonely dirty dogs like soot, wander around the dark,
Motionless roads,
Dogs barking, whining and cautiously wagging their
Thin, bony tails in happiness,
The dogs eat everything in their sight,
Ranging from unwanted food to stolen food.

Rachel Cunio (10)
Lower Park Primary School, Poynton

The Wonderful World Of Lowry

A dark and gloomy morning,
The dirty grey clouds hang in the sky like heavy curtains.

The factories were absolutely steaming out dusty black smoke,
It filled the air with a drift of mist,
There was a little sound coming from around,
There was a smash and a bang from the windows,
There was a loud creepy creaky sound from the hinge on the door.

The abandoned dogs were strolling adventurously,
The other dogs were inspecting the pavement,
One dog was on a lead,
But this he did not need,
Some were sniffing for as long as an hour,
They did not care what they did,
As long as they were safe with their owner.

People were walking around slowly,
Some people looked very lonely,
Most of the people were gathering to chatter,
The people looked very cold, cold as the snow,
People were hobbling across the road, one way street,
As some people were walking to meet the other people.

In the street, the clocks were ticking,
The wet damp church bell's ringing,
The pavement was uneven,
Some of the houses were colossal,
The lamp was as tall as a baby giraffe,
The steep steps were as slippy as a melted lollipop.

Georgie Clayton (10)
Lower Park Primary School, Poynton

Lowry's World!

Shabby dogs are looking longingly,
Like the howling wind,
Rough dogs are mongrels,
Ripping up a small
Scrap of meat
The size of a rat,
The lazy dogs were
Dawdling carelessly,
Small strange dogs
Were mysteriously exploring,
Some dogs were
Strolling calmly,
Jealous dogs were
Wandering silently,
Proud dogs were
Prowling majestically,
Wild dogs were nervously
Panting down the dark
Gloomy alleyway.

Most of the people wear
Dull clothes,
Men wore formal
Black top hats,
All of the matchstick
Men wore large shoes,
Lots of people wore
Old-fashioned clothes,
Some people were
Bulging out of their clothes,
Chubby children walk,
The cold icy roads.

The houses were as dull
As the midnight sky,
The drizzling rain slowly,
Patterns on the bumpy pavement,
Dark alleyways are
Littered with rubbish,
Shabby streets,
Roam the town,
The pavement is
As bumpy as the moon.

The thick black smoke
Is piping out of the tree like chimneys,
Smoke contaminating the polluted air,
The shapes of the factories are unusual,
Thick chimneys let out choking smoke,
A factory stands alone
In the freezing cold.

Sophie Hudson & Francesca Parrot
Lower Park Primary School, Poynton

Lowry Poem

Dogs slowly strolling in the cool breeze,
Lonely as an echoing scream,
They wander around not knowing where to go.

Steep steps covered in dust cold as stone,
Damp rotting doors still intact,
The dull lamp post alone as a stranger in the busy atmosphere.

The tall factories block out the light of the warm sun,
The factories smothered in coal pollute the air even more.

The ill people wander round looking for warmth,
Dull the small clothing they wear, with patches as dark as black paint.

Victoria Booth (9)
Lower Park Primary School, Poynton

Lowry's World

Lowry's world is dark and grey,
As children stroll down the street again,
Dogs are fighting for tiny meat scraps,
The dustbins are filled with rampaging rats.

Children are running around in the dark,
Adults silently strolling in the park,
The strange shaped houses alone in the street,
Just to have a home, is the greatest treat.

The streets are covered in rubbish and food,
The smoky atmosphere darkens the mood,
Thick smoke polluting the air,
When you look round, you see dark smoke everywhere.

Factories like a cold dark stone,
Dogs are howling looking for their home,
Men are swearing and staring sourly,
Frozen in the art of L S Lowry.

No wife, no pets,
Not even a cat,
So he never needs to rush,
He sits in the distance,
Alone in the darkness,
With only some paints and a brush.

Georgia Clay (10)
Lower Park Primary School, Poynton

Fun

Fun is baby blue like a children's toy,
It sounds like children laughing with joy,
It smells like my mum's freshly baked chocolate cake,
It looks like a medium sized play ball,
It feels like the smooth ripple of waves,
It reminds me of people bouncing on a trampoline.

Tom Holmes (8)
Lower Park Primary School, Poynton

Lowry's Picture

Lowry's picture is cold and dark,
People wandering in the park,
Smoke seeping from chimneys up high,
Murky clouds in the sky.

Factories polluting the misty air,
But nobody seems to really care,
Dark houses a treat to live in,
While the poor and unlucky get food from a bin.

Stray dogs with nowhere to go,
Who are lonely, lost and want to know,
Who are their owners and where they are,
They could be near but could be far.

Who would want to live here? I have no clue,
I wouldn't but would you?
The poor are as dirty as a sewer, it isn't fair,
If I were to live here, it would give me a scare.

I don't know why Lowry likes it here,
'It is great to paint,' I hear,
As well as collecting rent, he loved to paint,
His drawings were bold, certainly not faint.

Poppy Plumb (10)
Lower Park Primary School, Poynton

Happiness

Happiness is like a shimmering silver star in the dark sky,
It sounds like the rain pouring on the roof of the house,
It smells of poppies growing in the sun outside,
It looks like the sun shimmering in the blue sky,
It feels like the wind brushing against your face,
It reminds me of the seaside.

Alicia Vermeulen (9)
Lower Park Primary School, Poynton

The Lowry

The smelly factory coughing out smoke through
The tall chimneys like a man with a cold,
The tall, dark smoke flowing out of the factory,
Polluting the air of Salford,
The tall, towering weird shaped houses along the long,
Winding streets of smoky Salford.

The cold, damp stone steps lead up to the small terrace houses,
The lamp post as dull and dark as the cold
Night sky in the frosty December.

The dull-shaped people that only see the polluted air
And the factory's steamy, smokes,
Crouched over people plotted around looking like zombies.

The thin dogs wander aimlessly around the dirty pavements,
Trying to dodge their idiotic owners,
The black dogs paddling along with no owners.

Katie Sharrocks (9)
Lower Park Primary School, Poynton

Industrial Production

An industrial production happens all around you,
Dogs are darting for good scraps of food.

People are on their way to work,
Everyone has a place or thing to go to or from,
A scared and petrified man hides behind a wall,
What is he hiding from? Nobody knows.

Big street steps, steep and tall,
People talk about the weather and all,
Some are good and some are bad,
But most of them are bad.

Factories send out hoards of smoke,
Which make people choke,
But what we will never ever forget is . . .
Lawrence Stephen Lowry.

Joshua Edmunds
Lower Park Primary School, Poynton

Lowry's Life

The pram is as cosy as a fluffy blanket,
People plodding around like a herd of elephants,
It must be bitterly cold because most people are wearing hats,
Most pedestrians have got narrow slim flimsy legs.

One dog is striding aimlessly down the wet old alleyway,
The dogs are dashing rapidly across the bumpy road
                                            with their guardian,
There is a deserted dog without a leader or lead,
The ragged fur got caught in the light wind.

There is a church steeple in the gloomy distance,
As tall as a skyscraper,
There is a luminous lamp post as tall as a rocky mountain,
The top of the sky is as black and misty as the night sky,
There are many silver old metal railings and gates.

There is a very gloomy smoky sky
(that is why all the birds went to a cleaner environment),
There is loads of smoke beaming out of the chimneys,
Lots of chimneys with puffs of smoke coming out,
Dangerous chemicals fill the air,
(another reason why the birds left).

Louis Davies (9)
Lower Park Primary School, Poynton

Lowry's Life

Matchstick men walking down the dark, dull alleyways,
They are all wearing gloomy clothing,
The dim people strolling sadly.

The factories are full with black smoke,
Lots of gloomy factories.

Thick chimneys letting out choking smoke,
Smoke contaminating the air,
The lazy dogs are dawdling carelessly,
Some dogs are strolling calmly.

Charlie Kershaw (9)
Lower Park Primary School, Poynton

Well Done Mr Elephant!

He sits in the distance,
Alone in the darkness,
With only some paints and a brush,
The elephant is on his way to the fair,
So everyone is in a rush.

He's painting the background,
Of the animal parade,
What an important job,
But on his way to the colourful parade,
He is trampled by an angry mob.

Oh what shall I do,
He sits, he cries,
Then he has a great idea,
I know what I should do right now,
I need to face my fears.

So he sets down to work,
And starts brushing away,
Why didn't he think of it before?
All he has to do is paint his home,
Now the parade isn't a bore.

But it still isn't right,
Something's missing,
Oh yeah it is the bears,
But the animals are already walking down,
The bright road in laughing pairs.

Everyone is shouting,
I really don't know why,
Maybe cause the weather is bad,
But the elephant can't get through the crowd,
Because everyone is going mad.

They are not upset,
They are not unhappy,
Why then they are screaming,
I know, a tree has fallen over,
Cutting off the streaming.

But thankfully,
Mr Elephant's here,
He's here to save the day,
He lifts the tree, though it is very heavy,
Now everyone can run round and play.

Georgia Clay & Georgie Clayton (10)
Lower Park Primary School, Poynton

Lowry's World

The dogs are as thin as a twig on a tall tree,
Leadless dogs strolling about and sniffing,
The dogs are as black as a misty coal fire,
Many of the dogs are strays and are very lonely.

The pram is like a duck on wheels,
A man is hiding behind a rocky wall,
People talking very posh like the queen,
Old-fashioned clothing as black as a blackboard.

The factories are as dull and misty as the black night sky,
Big black smoke is like misty clouds when it's raining,
The fabric filthy factories are noisy day and night,
In the factory it is dirty and messy.

The dull pavements are as bumpy as coral reef and
As long and wiggly as a slithering snake,
Dull and misty streets are like coal in a fireplace,
Strange shaped houses are circular as a pillar
And as pointy as a pin.

Céline Sayers (9)
Lower Park Primary School, Poynton

Lowry's Autumn

Old people walk in dirty dusty clothes,
Pedestrians plod slowly through the black tarnished town,
The fellows do never split up,
Men never walk fast through the town.

Nobody goes down the spooky dark side of streets,
The bright bike shimmers through the misty night streets,
The lamp post shines in the distance,
The mouldy banner about to fall down from the rusty pole.

The dogs plod delicately down the grubby alley,
The soft dog strolled down the creepy side street,
The ragged fur of the dog got tangled as
He runs through the night wind,
The hopeless dog all sooty and dirty lay down on the grotty road.

There are dirty factories that give out thick smoke,
The grabby sooty dusty factories stand at the end of the street,
You could see through the old factory windows,
There were people washing dark coloured dogs,
Smoke pours out of the top of the factories.

Amy Warner (10)
Lower Park Primary School, Poynton

Darkness

Darkness is grey, darkness is black,
It sounds like thunder that stops you in your tracks,
It's as smelly as Marmite if you catch a whiff,
You see pitch-black and it stops you stiff,
I feel sad if it creeps up on me,
It reminds me of a bare no-leaved tree.

Katie Grimsditch (8)
Lower Park Primary School, Poynton

Lowry's Life

The grubby sooty factories stand at the end of the street alone,
Old people walk with dirty dusty clothes,
Pedestrians plod slowly through the dark tarnished town,
The misty lamp post shone in the smoky street.

The smoky atmosphere fills the sky with great darkness,
The bright bike shimmers in the foggy street,
The elderly spooky people stroll through the street,
The young baby cries out loud in his pram
As his mother pushes him along the cracked bumpy pavement.

The friendless hopeless dog all sooty and dirty
Lay down on the steep step,
The rough fur of the dog gets tangled as he
                            gallops through the street,
The dogs plod delicately down the grubby street,
The soft dog plodded down the cracked street.

Nobody goes to the dark spooky side street,
The dogs with no collars walk ham-fisted along the busy roads,
The smoke pours out from the top of the factories,
The mouldy banner hangs from the rusty poles about to fall down.

Kay Hoyle (9)
Lower Park Primary School, Poynton

Silence

Silence is navy like a torch shining through a dimly lit room,
It sounds like the golden flames crackling in the moonlight,
It smells like a muffin that's still hot and on its tray,
It looks like a flower on a twinkling summer's day,
It feels like a beanbag sitting in a room,
It reminds me of a beach with a slowly swirling sea.

Sarah Brighton (8)
Lower Park Primary School, Poynton

My Lowry Poem

The old people stroll slowly though the gloomy town,
The elderly people walk back bent in their smoky clothes,
The young baby cries out loud while their mum pushes them
In their pram,
The sound of the children playing in the distance.

The soft dog plodded down the cracked pavements,
The rough fur of the dogs get tangled as he gallops down the street,
The hopeless dog all sooty and dirty lay down on the slippery step.

The mouldy banner about to fall down,
The bright bike shimmering in the foggy street,
The misty lamp post shined in the smoky street,
The smoky atmosphere fills the air with great darkness.

The grubby dirty factories stand at the end of the street,
Smoky chimneys that pullute the air.

Laura Boldison (9)
Lower Park Primary School, Poynton

Happiness

Happiness is golden like a glistening treasure chest,
It sounds like a whale calling to his friends,
It smells of a mermaid, who is in a pile of diamonds,
It looks like my mum's face in a heap of stars,
It feels like a cute, little kitten who lets you stroke her,
It reminds me of my dog when he was a puppy
Chasing a butterfly.

Joseph Mullin (9)
Lower Park Primary School, Poynton

The Mysterious Man

A long row of houses alone in the streets,
With smoke pouring out of the foggy factory gates,
There he is. The mysterious man,
Painting in the distance.

He sits alone, a hat and a paintbrush,
No mum or dad, no sisters or brothers,
Not even a wife to care for.

His room is as empty as the night sky,
Full of rosette paintings,
He looks out of the window into his mild and misty world.

What does he do? No one will ever know,
Alone in the streets all day,
He paints a picture, a portrait of Anne,
He hopes he will meet the perfect lady some day.

A hat, a cloak and a heart.

Molly Blythe & Georgie Blears
Lower Park Primary School, Poynton

Happiness

Happiness is like the colour of bright yellow like the shimmering sun,
It smells of a scented candle burning in a bathroom,
It sounds like waves crashing against the rocks,
It looks like a little lamb bouncing around in circles, in a field,
It reminds me of a lovely roast dinner on a Sunday night.

Sophie Decker (8)
Lower Park Primary School, Poynton

The Town With No Name

The tall towering weird shaped houses along,
Long and winding streets of smoky Salford,
Freezing cold damp steps lead to small terrace houses,
The lamp posts are as dark as the night sky in December.

Tall, dark, smoky and black factory polluting the air,
The smelly factory coughing out smoke like a man with a bad cold.

People are walking around looking like zombies,
Dull people walking slowly in the polluted air.

Dogs trot along aimlessly in the thick polluted streets
Without their owners.

Otto Millard (10)
Lower Park Primary School, Poynton

At The Town Centre

In Lowry's loathsome world,
Whilst people rush to work,
Dogs dart trying to find scraps,
Factories pollute like mad,
Dogs eat scraps whilst people fight,
People hide, people run,
But no one is happy,
A lady rocks her pram,
People gather to talk,
The sky is dark,
People rush back and forth,
All the steps are uneven,
Smoke chokes people,
Damp doors crumble,
The streets are foggy,
In Lowry's loathsome world.

Sam Booth (9)
Lower Park Primary School, Poynton

L S Lowry

The dozy dogs scavenging for scraps of meat,
The dogs strolling proudly off their leads,
The greyhounds are as thin as Egyptian papyrus,
Dogs are trotting along next to their owners.

In the smelly, smoky town's people walk droopily in the polluted air,
Big factories cover the fields,
The fearless factories are as gloomy as the night sky,
The workers pile into the boring factories.

The bikes are as lonely as a tramp,
People stare at one legged people wheeling in their wheelchairs,
Babies crying in their prams,
Tramps eating out of garbage cans.

The houses are as dull covered as 1721 photos,
The houses are all different shapes and sizes,
The wire flows through the mysterious, misty air,
You can hear the church bells ringing.

Louis Evans (9)
Lower Park Primary School, Poynton

Fun

Fun is platinum like a glimmering medal,
It sounds like a rabbit sniffing in the snow,
It smells like hot dogs roasting in the oven,
It looks as if it is a roadrunner in the ice,
It feels much more of a smooth petal of a bright rose,
It reminds me of the beautiful butterfly in the forest.

Jayme Leigh (8)
Lower Park Primary School, Poynton

Fun

Fun is like a light blue ball bouncing on the ground,
It sounds like people laughing all through the night,
It smells like butter melting in a pot (a pound or two would do),
It looks like water swishing in a pot, it looks so white,
Fun feels like cream fresh from the pot or two,
Fun reminds me of flying a kite.

Holly McDowell (9)
Lower Park Primary School, Poynton

Sadness

Sadness is dark red like blood,
Sadness sounds tearful like a boy crying,
Sadness smells dead like a bullet from a gun,
Sadness looks horrid like a shot deer,
Sadness feels weird like a long car journey,
Sadness reminds me of my dead grandad.

Kyran Noone (8)
Lower Park Primary School, Poynton

Fun

Fun is platinum like a gleaming star,
It sounds like a golden eagle squawking,
Fun smells like the fresh air of the sky,
Fun looks like the stars twinkling in the night sky,
It feels like the wind of the high sea
And it reminds me of children playing.

Sam Doherty (8)
Lower Park Primary School, Poynton

I'm Not Too Keen On School

I'm not too keen on school,
Some people think it's really cool,
The corridors are always squeaky clean,
And plus all of the teachers are really mean,
Maths, literacy gotta be the worst subjects ever,
But sometimes I'm really clever,
My favourite subject's gotta be lunch,
So I can munch and crunch,
At the end of the day,
Everyone jumps and shouts 'hooray!'
I thought to myself,
That wasn't so bad after all,
I think I'll come back next fall.

Lauren Vaughan (10)
Newton Primary School, Chester

Back To School

Back to school is so boring,
Teacher's got to stop us snoring,
Work is just so uncool,
We want to go to the swimming pool.

On the playground we are found
Eating snacks and racing round.

Munch, munch, crunch, crunch.
Munch, munch, crunch, crunch.

Now it's nearly time to go, got to run and say hello.

Teacher, teacher don't be late,
Our mums are waiting at the gate.

India Darlington, Sian Roszich (9), Zoe Goulding
& Natasha Cooksley
Newton Primary School, Chester

I Wish!

I wish I could travel through time and space,
Like explorers and travellers, through time I would race,
I'd meet Doctor Who and maybe K9,
I'd be their best friend and they would be mine,
I'd love to see all the planets and stars,
Like Jupiter, Venus, Neptune and Mars,
I'd zip past some aliens from the Milky Way,
I'd fly in my rocket all night and all day,
If I could blast off to travel through space,
I'd vanish right now and not leave a trace,
Travelling through space would be so brill,
Amazing, fantastic, just great,
Such a thrill.

Courtney Roberts
Newton Primary School, Chester

Birthdays All Around The World

B rilliant presents from friends and family,
I love gifts because they are beautiful,
R eally exciting parties,
T housands and thousands of cards,
H appy smiling people playing,
D iscos put on and making lots of noise,
A nother year gone by, another year older,
Y ou are the luckiest person for the day.
S miles and laughter, fun and friendship,
  That's what birthdays are.

Jessica Proctor Crozier (7)
Newton Primary School, Chester

Fizzy Drinks

Coca Cola,
7-Up,
Pour it out into a cup,
Lemonade,
Cherryade,
Do you know how they are made?
Fanta,
Water,
Sunny D,
You can't drink it, it's just for me,
There's many more drinks that we could tell,
Apple juice,
Orange juice,
We know so well.

Molly McBride (8)
Newton Primary School, Chester

All About Me

My name is Emma,
I have lots of friends,
We play together,
Our friendship never ends,
Skipping, basketball is what we play,
We play together every day,
My best friends Aylin, Antonia too,
We like playing something new,
When we get home, I ask if they can play,
Maybe a sleepover but please can they stay?
And that's all about me.

Emma Reynolds (9)
Newton Primary School, Chester

Sunset

The tangerine sunset fell as slowly as ever,
Below the tips of the tallest trees.

People gazed with wonder as they followed the lines
Of gold flicker down the sky.

It was just like a melting rainbow of different colours,
Fading away to the darkness of the night sky.

A moonlight night was approaching,
A white, creamy moon surrounded by pools of darkness.

Georgina Guy (11)
Newton Primary School, Chester

Ocean Delight

The salty air invaded my senses,
As I watched the mighty waves crash on the shore,
Clever clams clung to the rocks,
As daring dolphins dived into the deep blue.

The crafty crabs darted from pool to pool,
Whilst wonderful whales sang their praises,
It was as though I was in paradise,
How I dream of staying by the sea forever.

Gabriella Biasillo (8)
Newton Primary School, Chester

Happiness Is . . .

My dog,
My fish,
My friends,
My family,
Is after school,
Is home!

Saskia Caley (9)
Onchan Primary School, Douglas

I Am . . .

I am as ticklish as an elephant,
I am a shopping queen,
I can't keep away from chocolate,
I am a sport champion.

I am a gold medal champion,
I am one of Caitlin's best friends,
I am more glittery than the stars,
I am brighter than the sun.

Katie Garrett (9)
Onchan Primary School, Douglas

Happiness Is . . .

Playing football,
Watching TV at home,
Playing on the PlayStation 2,
Listening to music,
Going on holiday,
When it's my birthday,
When it's Christmas.

Jacob Jones (9)
Onchan Primary School, Douglas

The Sea

The waves crashing,
The sand crunching,
The thunder bashing,
The fishes munching.

Zoe Davidson (9)
Onchan Primary School, Douglas

Happiness Is . . .

Seeing something pink,
Playing on my pink Nintendo DS Lite,
Having very good friends,
Clothes shopping with my mum,
Putting make-up on,
Dancing with my best friend Zoe,
Watching TV in bed,
Going on a cool and fun holiday,
Skipping on the fields with my friends,
Playing netball and badminton.

Charlotte Cunningham (9)
Onchan Primary School, Douglas

Kitchen

The screeching baby, wa, wa, wa,
The sound of the children moaning,
The noise of the popping cornflakes,
Pop, pop, pop,
The screeching noise of the flying toast.

Caitlin Hutton (9)
Onchan Primary School, Douglas

Happiness Is

School disco,
Playing football,
Going on my PS2,
Watching a new film,
Birthdays
And going on holiday.

Yohann Williamson (9)
Onchan Primary School, Douglas

Sounds Of The World

Ruff, ruff, went the dog passing by,
Miaow, miaow, went the cat with the guy,
Hop, hop, went the bunny,
Ha, ha, it looked kind of funny.

Click, clack, went a pair of high heels,
Crunch, crunch, went a man eating a meal,
Tick-tock, went the clock in the Town Hall,
Bye- bye, I heard the people call.

Stacey Clarke (10)
Onchan Primary School, Douglas

The Horse Is In The Stable

Horses in their stables,
Crunch, crunch, crunch,
The switch in the lights,
Click, click, click,
The hay in their mouths,
Munch, munch, munch.

Hannah Louise Frost (9)
Onchan Primary School, Douglas

Can You Score A Goal?

The fans cheering when the footballer scores a goal,
The zooming of the car,
Then the football goes again,
It flies very far,
And you would never guess, it just hit the bar.

Lewis Croft (9)
Onchan Primary School, Douglas

Sounds Of Life

The granny snoring, *aah ooo aah ooo aah ooo,*
The train moving, *choo, choo, choo,*
The dishwasher pinging, *ping, ping, ping,*
The telephone ringing, *ring, ring, ring.*

The sink bubbling, *bubble, bubble, bubble,*
The pizza tower wobbling, *wobble, wobble, wobble,*
The cowbells clanging, *clang, clang, clang,*
The drumbeat banging, *bang, bang, bang.*

The windowpanes rattling, *rattle, rattle, rattle,*
The baby babbling, *babble, babble, babble,*
The Ferrari vrooming, *vroom, vroom, vroom,*
The stereo booming, *boom, boom, boom.*

Jonathan Kneale (9)
Onchan Primary School, Douglas

Nature

The screech of the peregrine living in Onch,
The snarl of a tiger, prey in reach,
The raven goes cronk,
The ringed plover wailing on the beach.

Glug of a chub far away,
Miaow of a stray,
The blackbird tweeting,
Flocks of redwings seeping.

Creep of a spider,
The birch sounding free,
The warbler starts to warble,
The kingfisher singing with glee.

Adam Peet (9)
Onchan Primary School, Douglas

Colour, Colour . . .

Colour, colour everywhere,
Makes you stand,
Makes you stare.

Fire is the colour red
It keeps you warm
When in your bed.

Colour, colour everywhere,
Makes you stand,
Makes you stare.

The sea is blue and salty too
There are loads of fishes
Swimming through.

Colour, colour everywhere,
Makes you stand,
Makes you stare.

Grass is green, grass is blue,
Everton,
Yahoo!

Colour, colour everywhere,
Makes you stand,
Makes you stare.

Lewis Humphreys (7)
St Brigid's RC Primary School, Knowsley

Tell Me . . .

Tell me, tell me,
Tell me now.
Where and when
And who and how?

Why are lemons so sweet?
Why does everyone have two feet?

Tell me, tell me,
Tell me now.
Where and when
And who and how?

Why is the sun so yellow?
Why is a man called a fellow?

Tell me, tell me,
Tell me now.
Where and when
And who and how?

Why is the light so bright?
Why is the rope on a kite so tight?

Tell me, tell me,
Tell me now.
Where and when
And who and how?

Aaron Towner (7)
St Brigid's RC Primary School, Knowsley

Colour, Colour . . .

Colour, colour everywhere,
Makes you stand,
Makes you stare.

Fire is the colour red
It keeps you warm
When in your bed.

Colour, colour everywhere,
Makes you stand,
Makes you stare.

The sea is blue and salty too
There's loads of fishes
Swimming through.

Colour, colour everywhere,
Makes you stand,
Makes you stare.

Grass is green, it makes me sneeze
It grows and grows
In the lovely breeze.

Colour, colour everywhere,
Makes you stand,
Makes you stare.

Jordanna Shelbourne (7)
St Brigid's RC Primary School, Knowsley

Colour, Colour . . .

Colour, colour everywhere,
Makes you stand,
Makes you stare.

Fire is the colour red
It keeps you warm
When in bed.

Colour, colour everywhere,
Makes you stand,
Makes you stare.

The sea is blue and salty too,
There's loads of fishes
Swimming through.

Colour, colour everywhere,
Makes you stand,
Makes you stare.

The sun is yellow in the sky
It shines all day
I want to fly.

Colour, colour everywhere,
Makes you stand,
Makes you stare.

Erin Ellis (7)
St Brigid's RC Primary School, Knowsley

Colour, Colour . . .

Colour, colour everywhere,
Makes you stand,
Makes you stare.

Fire is the colour red
It keeps you warm
When in your bed.

Colour, colour everywhere,
Makes you stand,
Makes you stare.

The sea is blue and salty too
There's loads of fishes
Swimming through.

Colour, colour everywhere,
Makes you stand,
Makes you stare.

Grass is green it sways and sways
It's long and short
And sways different ways.

Colour, colour everywhere,
Makes you stand,
Makes you stare.

Keavy Christian (7)
St Brigid's RC Primary School, Knowsley

Tell Me, Tell Me . . .

Tell me, tell me,
Tell me now.
Where and when
And who and how?

Why are lemons so sweet?
Why does everyone have to feet.

Tell me, tell me,
Tell me now.
Where and when
And who and how.

Why do boys play football?
Why do we eat in the hall?

Tell me, tell me,
Tell me now.
Where and when
And who and how?

Why is the sun so bright?
Why do tigers always bite?

Tell me, tell me,
Tell me now.
Where and when
And who and how?

Morgan Povey (8)
St Brigid's RC Primary School, Knowsley

School, School . . .

School, school where you have lots of fun
School, school where the work's never done.

I have a cup at dinner time
During literacy we make a rhyme.

School, school where you have lots of fun,
School, school where the work's never done.

In December when it's Christmas time
We always have a pantomime.

School, school where you have lots of fun,
School, school where the work's never done.

We have assembly in the hall,
In PE we throw balls.

School, school where you have lots of fun,
School, school where the work's never done.

Every day we have school dinner,
If you don't eat it you get thinner.

School, school where you have lots of fun,
School, school where the work's never done.

School, school, the girls are very cool!

Mia Grimes (7)
St Brigid's RC Primary School, Knowsley

School, School . . .

School, school, where you have lots o fun,
School, school, where the work's never done.
Where the teachers always moan,
Mr Fleming's on the phone.

School, school, where you have lots of fun,
School, school, where the work's never done.
The teachers have their tea in a cup,
If you don't bring your homework in, they'll eat you all up.

School, school, where you have lots of fun,
School, school, where the work's never done.
At special times we have a mass,
But then we go back to class.

School, school, where you have lots of fun,
School, school, where the work's never done.

Megan Farrington (7)
St Brigid's RC Primary School, Knowsley

Our Schooldays

Dressing up days are really cool,
Even though some of us look a fool.
We really like coming to school,
Because we know that it is cool.
Laughing and playing in the sun,
Hopping and skipping, having so much fun.

Our clubs at school are cool,
But we don't have a swimming pool.
Football is a popular sport,
Although rounders is just like running to ports.
Rugby club to keep you fit,
Book club if you want to read and sit.
Although some children blub if they don't get into the club!

Our School dinners really rock,
All the others taste like a sock.
Our school dinners are really yummy,
Everything really fills our tummy.
All the food is good for you,
Gives you energy for the work you do.

You might be good at football,
You might be good at track,
But when it comes to basketball
You might as well step back.
Go on step back,
You might as well do that!

St John's CE Primary School Book Club
St John's CE Primary School, Sandbach

The River

The river is a sly Jaguar,
Unpredictable and strong,
He rushes down the gorge all day long,
With his flesh shredding teeth and sneaky thinking,
Year upon year he can't stop killing,
The clueless, helpless prey,
And away, away, away, away,
The angry river cat begins to say,
His itchy head scratching.

And when the evening breeze is whistling,
When the moon reappears in the misty sky,
He jumps to attention and prowls and prowls,
Through the jungle he dances,
And groans and growls long and hard.

But on calmer days in the sunny weeks,
When even the smallest of birds stuff their beaks,
Instead of screaming their scared shriek,
With the sun on his back,
He'd never attack,
Silent, so silent, he can only relax.

Sean Clarke (10)
SS Peter & Paul RC Primary School, Wallasey

Guilt

Guilt is the colour of deep, dark black, a deep dark
Feeling that shivers up your back.
Guilt, it looks like this, a giant spider attacking you in
A fright, in the middle of the night.
Guilt sounds like a howl and a moan from a wolf,
As it gazes at the moon.
Guilt feels like the sea, crashing into the rocks,
Guilt it tastes like stinky cheese from a year ago,
Guilt smells like smoke, spitting out of the exhaust pipe
Of an old banger.

Josephine Ruiz (9)
SS Peter & Paul RC Primary School, Wallasey

Shivers

Bushes quiver,
Where shadows lean,
And not a sliver,
Of moon is seen.

Near the river,
Some goblins (green)
With a witch in front,
And a ghost in-between.

Make me sh . . . i . . . . vvver,
But I am keen,
About the shivers
Of Hallowe'en,
And black as a bat,
With stringy long hair,
Where his head was flat.

The sad little ghost,
Didn't want any hair,
Or a black pointed hat,
So he said, 'Witch beware!'
Then he chanted some words,
With a spell-casting switch,
And gave Hallowe'en Night,
A bald-headed witch!

Hafiza Brepotra (10)
SS Peter & Paul RC Primary School, Wallasey

Grumpiness

Grumpiness is grey like a stampeding elephant,
Grumpiness looks like a big frown,
Grumpiness sounds like a shouting man,
Grumpiness feels bumpy like rough sandpaper,
Grumpiness tastes like a loaf of chewy, stale bread,
Grumpiness smells like mouldy cheese.

Gabriel Pillitteri (9)
SS Peter & Paul RC Primary School, Wallasey

A Tornado

A tornado is a roaring lion,
Loud and fierce,
It swirls over the land for days,
With his humungous claws and bulging eyes,
Day upon day he sighs,
The mumbling, bumbling tune,
Of 'Food, food, food, food!'
The large tornado - lion moans,
Licking his hungry lips.

And when the stormy wind hits
And the trees bend in the rain
It pounces on the unsuspecting prey,
Ripping them apart chewing up anything in the way,
And growls and groans loud and proud.

But when it moves on, stomach dragging on the ground,
It leaves behind a terrible mound,
With bits of prey scattered around,
It slinks off back where it came,
To sleep calmly away from sight,
Waiting, waiting to pounce again.

Alastair Nokes (10)
SS Peter & Paul RC Primary School, Wallasey

The Sea Dog

The waves crash as the sea dog howls,
The seaweed floats as he moans,
The thunder strikes as he splashes,
The waves grow bigger as he becomes angry,
The tide goes in and out as the sea dog drags his claws
Along the seabed floors,
The sea dog becomes darker as the wind gets stronger,
As the boat gets near, the sailors have more fear,
Why oh why are you so fearsome and deadly?

Alexandra Smith (10)
SS Peter & Paul RC Primary School, Wallasey

The Ocean

The ocean is a white horse,
Powerful and swift,
She stamps on the shores in temper,
With her sparkling mane and swishing tail,
Year upon year she sails,
The tumbling, crumbling waves,
And 'caves, caves, caves, caves!'
The powerful white horse craves,
Rolling her glistening eyes.

And when the stormy wind howls,
And lightning dances in stormy sky,
She gallops in whirling whirlpools,
Leaping and laughing in the cools,
And creeps and leaps, slick and sly.

But on quiet days in April or May,
When even the seabirds have nothing to say,
Each and every day,
With her breath, steady and calm,
The stillness soothing like a balm,
So still, so still the silences charm.

Bethany Fleming (10)
SS Peter & Paul RC Primary School, Wallasey

Anger

The colour of anger is red,
It looks like burnt candy,
The sound of anger is like
A wounded banshee, crying in pain,
Anger feels like my head is about to explode,
Like a volcano about to erupt,
Anger tastes like rotten milk and mouldy cheese,
Anger smells like sweaty chips which makes
Me want to sneeze,
I don't like anger, do you?

Philip McGarry (10)
SS Peter & Paul RC Primary School, Wallasey

The Ocean

The ocean is a white horse,
Stamping and snorting,
She kicks on the shore with anger,
With her greedy eyes and frightening snorts,
Hour upon hour she talks
To the swishing, swaying sand,
And 'friends, friends, friends!'
The white horse moans,
Kicking the silky sand.

And when the night wind roars,
And the moon rocks in the stormy cloud,
She bounds to her hooves and snorts and sways,
Shaking a sandy mane over the sea,
And neighs and neighs, long and loud.

But on quiet days in May or June,
When even the grasses on the dune
Play no more their reedy tune,
With her head between her hooves,
She lies on the sandy shores,
So quiet, so quiet, she scarcely snorts.

Catherine Braidwood-Harrington (10)
SS Peter & Paul RC Primary School, Wallasey

The Sea

The sea is an angry dog,
He crashes against the rocks like a big boxer,
Sometimes on sunny days he is very calm,
He leaves pools like shiny mirrors as he goes to and fro,
On the hot, rippling sand,
Ships sink into his deep, dark black mouth
When he is hungry,
When he is angry, only the fish know how to calm him down,
But that secret lies only with the tropical fish.

Holly Anne Lyas (9)
SS Peter & Paul RC Primary School, Wallasey

Fire

Fire is a towering tiger,
Leaping and roaring,
He burns in the forest all day long,
With his gnashing teeth and sharp claws,
Day after day he angrily roars,
At the threatening sun,
And 'runs, runs, runs, runs!'
He darkly hums,
Licking his fiery paws.

And when the night air dampens,
And the fire flickers in the dark,
He dives into the embers and sparks and growls and cackles,
Stretching his limbs of the vegetation,
And yawns and purrs slowly and quietly.

But on winter days in November,
Forest fires commemorate the gunpowder plot,
The giant tiger awakens from his slumber,
And re-ignites,
So silent, he hungrily yawns.

Eleanor Regan (9)
SS Peter & Paul RC Primary School, Wallasey

The Sea

You are as blue as coral,
You are dangerous and wild,
Sometimes I can hear you sigh,
I don't understand your sadness,
You smash rocks like a boxer,
You are moody,
You remind me of sadness,
I collect your shells and eat your cockles,
I swim in your water,
I catch your fish,
You are the sea.

Joseph Swann (10)
SS Peter & Paul RC Primary School, Wallasey

The Eagle

The eagle is the swiftest bird,
Broad-winged and brown,
It rests in its nest all day,
With its mighty claws and beady eyes,
Higher and higher it flies into
The boiling and scorching sun,
And, 'fun, fun, fun, fun!'
The great eagle squawks,
Licking its dangerous beak,
And when the morning light shines,
And the sun moves into the thick clouds,
It flies down to the ground and twists and turns,
Stretching its wide wings over the burns,
And screeches and screams, long and loud,
But on silent days in the black night,
Whenever the snakes fight,
No more with their might,
With its wings covering its entire body,
It sleeps in its strong nest,
So peaceful, so peaceful, it quietly comes to rest.

Ben Murphy (10)
SS Peter & Paul RC Primary School, Wallasey

Love

Love is the colour the deep red of a beautiful rose,
Given for love,
Love is the smell of perfume, worn for a romantic meal,
Love is the taste of Belgian chocolates,
Filled with rich, chocolately cream,
Love feels like a soft feather,
Swooping through the air,
Love is the hug given to a teddy bear,
When going to sleep at night.

Michael Westcott (9)
SS Peter & Paul RC Primary School, Wallasey

The Sun

The sun is a fiery flame,
Wild and bright,
It shines in the sky all day,
With its blinding light and beaming lines,
Time upon time it shines,
The rumbling crumbling world,
And curled, curled, curled, curled!
The giant fire flame whirls,
Lighting his beaming lines.

And when the night wind roars,
And the sun lies down in the darkening sky,
He sleeps in the deep and sets and sinks,
And of its slumber long it thinks,
It dreams of tomorrow and soaring high.

But in the morning when all is still,
The sun comes up of its own freewill,
The rays creep out over the hill,
The sunbeams dance both high and low,
Creeping alone row by row,
It is nature's wondrous show.

Olivia Jones (10)
SS Peter & Paul RC Primary School, Wallasey

Monkey

Paraglider, banana finder,
Tree shaker, leaf raker,
Banana muncher, nut cruncher,

Noise maker, banana taker,
Banana peeler, great dealer,

Tree flyer, lazy lier,
Tree racer, banana chaser.

Cameron Bradley (9)
SS Peter & Paul RC Primary School, Wallasey

The Dragon Of The Sky

The thunder and lightning is a massive dragon, scaly and red,
He hides in the clouds all day,
With his flaring nostrils and smoky breath,
Night after night, he brings death,
To the defenceless, helpless city,
And 'pity, pity, pity, pity!'
The giant dragon laughs,
Bellowing his booming calls.

And when the rain calls,
And the moon appears in grey clouds,
He sneaks off the clouds and rages and roars,
Smacking his humungous jaws,
And strikes and smashes violently and ferociously,
But on warm days in summer or spring,
When even the rain cannot be king.

Raging storms are not the thing,
With his fluffy clouds,
So silent, so silent, he sleeps so sound.

Katie Ann Clarke (9)
SS Peter & Paul RC Primary School, Wallasey

Love

Love is the colour pink,
Love looks like a heart flying in the air,
Love sounds like the sea swishing in the wind,
Love feels like peace and happiness,
Love tastes like chocolate melting in your mouth,
Love smells like cookies baking in the oven,
Love is wonderful.

Megan Hynes (9)
SS Peter & Paul RC Primary School, Wallasey

Droughts

A drought is a scorching heat,
Blitzful and deadly,
It devastates the land without mercy,
With its deadly dryness and blinding light,
Month upon month, it fights,
The splishing, splashing rain,
And, 'away, away, away, away!'
The scorching heat says all day,
Shining its fierce light.

The weather is calm and mellow,
The atmosphere welcomes a change,
There is a shift of fury,
As he howls and bellows,
He gives hope to the shallows.

But when the clouds come in after a year or two,
And across the sky they flew and flew,
A patch of rain clouds then blew,
With it being so weak,
It's thunderclouds we seek,
And the heavenly rain, it happily leaks.

David Power (11)
SS Peter & Paul RC Primary School, Wallasey

Sadness

It sounds like one thousand screams,
It feels like never-ending torment,
It tastes like the world's sourest lemon,
It smells like an egg that has gone rotten,
Its colour is a murky dark blue, lost in the sky,
Sadness is horrible, I hate this feeling.

Ciaran Quinn (9)
SS Peter & Paul RC Primary School, Wallasey

Who Am I?

Door breaker,
Money taker,
Gun shooter,
Shoplifter,
Knife killer,
Pistol threatener,
Clothes stealer,
Police finder,
Cruel destroyer,
Handbag snatcher,
Runaway suspector,
Human killer,
Jewellery taker,
Sword threatener,
Window smasher,
Jail breaker . . .

Find the escaper.

Alex Davison (9)
SS Peter & Paul RC Primary School, Wallasey

The Sea

The sea is wild and hungry,
It is like a grey dog,
It can swallow anything in its path,
Sometimes, I hear you sigh,
You leave pools like pearls,
Your jaws are the waves that crash over me,
Your tides are like the pages of a book,
I don't understand your sadness,
You are as blue as coral,
You change the way you are, from day to day,
But then I hear your laughter roar,
And sometimes you are as silent as a fallen tree,
I see you every day.

Nadia Callister (9)
SS Peter & Paul RC Primary School, Wallasey

The Wind

The wind is an angry eagle, sly and quick,
It plans in the nest all night,
With his stalking fly and evil eye,
Hour upon hour he waits in the crashing, lashing sky,
And 'meat, meat, meat, meat!'
The angry eagle screeches licking his dirty beak.

When the night wind roars and the moon shines bright,
The eagle stirs and gets ready for flight,
Faster and faster, he flies to the ground
And captures a rabbit without a sound.

But on quiet days in May or June,
When even the lightest clouds don't move,
Nothing moves in the sky or on the ground.
The eagle is sleeping not making a sound,
So silent, so silent, but for how long?
When will he wake and become very strong?

Erin Adderley (9)
SS Peter & Paul RC Primary School, Wallasey

The Deep Blue Sea

The sea is like a big blue sheet
That tosses and turns,
The white horses run across your back,
But it doesn't seem to hurt,
The big white moon leads it to different places
With the ships on your back,
You are as deep as the dark blue coral
And full of emotion,
You sigh with sadness when you leave
The golden sand and shores,
You leave sparkly mirrors upon the shores,
I come every day to see you but you always sneak away.

Bethan Blanchfield (9)
SS Peter & Paul RC Primary School, Wallasey

The Mermaid

The mermaid is a mystical witch,
Modest and sly,
She plays on the rocks all day,
With her gleaming comb and sparkling shell,
Hour upon hour she sings,
Her enchanting, bewitching songs.

And when the heavy rain pours,
And the waves smash against the battered breakers,
She jumps into the sea and splish, splash,
Shaking her wet hair over the rocks,
She sings and screams loud and long.

But in the calmer days in the summer months,
When even the fish can't be seen -
Swim no more their snakish style,
She sits upon the rocks,
So still, so still, she scarcely breathes.

Marnie Melia (10)
SS Peter & Paul RC Primary School, Wallasey

Anger

Anger is the colour of bright red,
It looks like a bomb about to explode,
It sounds like an over-steaming kettle,
It feels like you want to throw something far away,
It tastes like rotten bacon,
It smells like milk that is off
And hasn't been opened in 10 years.

Christopher Williams (9)
SS Peter & Paul RC Primary School, Wallasey

The Crocodile

A puddle is a massive crocodile, long and scaly,
It runs on the mud all day,
With its smashing tail and humungous teeth,
Day after day it boils, the boiling scorching sun,
And 'fun, fun, fun, fun',
The giant crocodile bellows,
Throwing its massive tail.

And when the rain comes down,
And the sun hides in the clouds,
It jumps to its body and looks
As the humungous, dark clouds cook,
As it walks and moans large and loud.

But on rainy days when the waterfall comes down,
And the tiny drops of water,
Which makes people slaughter,
With its tail laid down,
It lies in the shaded town,
So silent, so silent, he finally comes down.

Georgina Murphy (9)
SS Peter & Paul RC Primary School, Wallasey

Sadness

Sadness tastes like a cold cup of tea,
On a really cold day,
Sadness smells like someone did something bad,
Sadness is a colour of grey on a rainy, muggy day,
Sadness looks like a tear falling down on your sad face,
Sadness sounds like a lamb that's lost from its mum,
Sadness feels like a cold-blooded fish on the beach.

Katie Gillespie (9)
SS Peter & Paul RC Primary School, Wallasey

School

School - boring,
Children - snoring,
Lunch - appalling,
Playground - adoring.

Teachers - stinking,
Head teacher - twitching,
Dinner ladies - snitching,
Caretaker - snoozing.

PE - amazing,
Maths - degrading,
Science - creepy,
English - sleepy.

Home time - nearing,
Classrooms - clearing,
Bell - ringing,
Children - singing.

Lucy Jones (9)
SS Peter & Paul RC Primary School, Wallasey

The Sea

You are as blue as the sky on a bright summer's day,
You are as silent as a feather as it gently floats away,
You smell like a single red rose, fresh and beautiful,
You are a wild lion,
You taste like cockles,
When I see you, I think of your water crashing against the rocks.

Jasmyn Doherty (11)
SS Peter & Paul RC Primary School, Wallasey

The Snow

The snow is a lonely leopard,
Wild and free,
It prowls in the mist all day,
With its ferocious jaws and heavy paws,
Day after day it lures,
The unsuspecting foraging fowl
And prowl, prowl, prowl, prowl,
The silent leopard howls,
Calling to the forest.

And when the violent blizzards spread,
And the sky drifts in the cloudy mist,
It jumps to its feet and stretches and lifts,
Dragging its smooth coat over the drifts,
And grizzles and growls short and swift.

But on peaceful days in June and July,
When even the snow is nigh,
Transforms the land with vegetation high,
With its head on a mound,
So peaceful, so peaceful, it hardly makes a sound.

Ella Mooney (10)
SS Peter & Paul RC Primary School, Wallasey

Loneliness

Loneliness feels like everyone has turned their back on you
And there is nobody to talk to,
It sounds like a tear hitting the ground, from your moody face,
It looks like someone living in a cardboard box,
It smells like eating food from your only plate,
It is the colour of the black in a light bulb when it goes out,
Loneliness will never be me because of my great family!

Luke Wellens (9)
SS Peter & Paul RC Primary School, Wallasey

The Car

A car is a powerful machine,
Big and bold,
It revs on the engine when it's cold,
With its fantastic V8 and brilliant speed,
Night upon night it leads,
The racing speeding cars,
And, 'stars, stars, stars, stars'!
The giant machine roars,
Cooling its engine down.

And when the night comes down,
And the headlamps pierce the dark,
It speeds down lanes and rums and rams,
Dodging the walls and hedges,
And rages and roars long and loud.

But on quiet days in May or June,
When even the hedges on the path,
Play no more their brushy tune,
With its nose between his wheels,
It rests on the drive stones,
So quiet, so quiet, it gently drones.

Lewis Kenwright (11)
SS Peter & Paul RC Primary School, Wallasey

Lightning

The lightning is a ferocious beast,
Dazzling but destructive,
It flashes in the field all night,
With its crackling noise and bashing storms,
Minute after minute it forms,
The raging, changing brute,
And, 'shoots, shoots, shoots, shoot'!
The great lightning flutes,
Watching the people mourn.

And when the sky lights up
And the landscape changes colour,
The forks reach out far and wide,
Crashing down on its side,
It snaps and cracks across the borough.

But when the storm passes by,
The air and clouds heave a sigh,
No more worries in the sky,
All is quiet, the lighting is gone,
The sun appears and the storm moves on,
So quiet, so calm, the sun has won.

Thomas McWilliam (10)
SS Peter & Paul RC Primary School, Wallasey

The Wolf

The wind is a howling wolf,
Quick and swift,
He paces through the forest all night,
With his fluffy fur and pointy ears,
Hour upon hour he fears,
The leaning, falling trees,
And, 'breeze, breeze, breeze, breeze',
The grey wolf moans,
Looking at the leaves,
And when the night wind roars,
And the sky is covered in clouds,
He jumps to his feet and scritches and scratches,
Licking his sore bare patches,
As he roars and bellows long and loud.

But on calm days in April and May,
Where people like to lie on the bay,
On the grass is where he lay,
With his back on the floor,
His patches are no longer sore,
He doesn't need to say anymore.

Esther Edwards (9)
SS Peter & Paul RC Primary School, Wallasey

Love

Love is the colour red and pink,
Love looks like melted chocolate,
And a big warm cup of milk,
Love sounds like romantic music,
Love feels as if you are under the moon and stars,
With your first love,
Love tastes like pink, fluffy candyfloss,
Love smells like red, red roses,
Love is in the shape of a heart and
The colour of beaming red and pink.

Niamh Oliveira (9)
SS Peter & Paul RC Primary School, Wallasey

My Life As A Football Boot

The closet was opened and light surrounded me,
I was picked up by my laces and carried into the car,
Then I was placed in a big red gym bag.
Suddenly the bag started to shake,
And my studs clicked and clacked on the bottom of the seat.
Next a sudden stop occurred to the wheeled roller coaster
And I was taken to the pitch.
The zip opened and I was put in the changing room
And I sat still for at least an hour.
Then out of nowhere, I was picked up
And me and my brother were put onto the feet.
All shoes of every kind hate the sweaty stench of the feet.
It is unbearable to the sole.
The whistle blew and I was heading for the ball.
The final score was one-nil to us
And a headache for me!

Patrick Hartney (10)
St Peter's Catholic Primary School, Stalybridge

Sun

Raven
He's big,
He is fast,
He is epic size,
Left us all in darkness.
He left all of us alone,
He left us all sad and scared,
He saved my very own life,
He put the sun back,
He saved our lives
We were safe once again
Home.

Matt O'Brien (10)
St Peter's Catholic Primary School, Stalybridge

My Life As A Christmas Tree

Freedom at last!
The attic door slowly creaked open,
Then a strong male lifted me down some clanking steps.
I was then left,
Standing in the corner of a dimly lit room.
All around me were children
With tinsel and fairy lights grasped in their eager little hands.
Then I spotted a woman with a box of tree decorations,
I knew what was going to happen next.

I was crying with misery,
On went the decorations.
Why oh why did they have to be so heavy?
I suddenly collapsed with the weight.
I heard children around me whimpering,
Surprised at my fall.

Then I felt a male lift me once again,
Out of a door,
Into a garden,
The cold was stinging me.
Then I was thrown on the top of a heap of rubbish.
I was left alone,
In the bitter snow.

I never saw my leaves again,
When a truck lifted me to my destiny.

And now I am,
If you haven't guessed,
This very piece of paper!

Cara Headdock (11)
St Peter's Catholic Primary School, Stalybridge

The Stolen Sun

The world was empty,
No one to talk to, no one to see,
Until the raven, glowing with glee,
Came down to Earth from his own land,
And created the sea and created the sand,
And all of the people and all of the plants
And all of the creatures like the tigers and ants.

But sadly, one day,
The people turned mean,
And violence like this had never been seen.
So Raven took action and flew away with the sun,
Then all of the people knew what they'd done.

Then months and months later,
A boy called Little Darkness found a mask in the water,
So he picked it up and placed it on his head,
Then all of a sudden he felt something heavy and said,
'Oh wow! I have wings growing on my back!'
He flew up to some glowing ice and started to hack
But then down swooped the raven and grabbed hold of the boy,
'Get away from that sun, it is not a toy!'
The words shocked the boy and he started to fall,
So the raven grabbed hold of him, and the large shining ball.
He then carried them down to the land of all snow,
Then threw the sun in the air, and it started to glow.
He placed the boy down and then flew away,
Then all the snow melted and they all cheered, 'Hooray!'

Sam Nero (11)
St Peter's Catholic Primary School, Stalybridge

My Life As a Peach

It was early in the morning,
The children were eating breakfast,
They were ready to go,
But then the children came closer to the fruit basket,
This was one thing all fruits hate,
Going to school with a human!

We drove slowly but time was going fast for me,
Soon I would be gone!
The car stopped - the bag I was in was lifted,
The child left me in the bag for some time.

The bell rang, so the time had come,
I would *die!*
I could ear the zip being unzipped,
A hand came in and grabbed me,
The hand took me out,
I could feel it squeezing me then, suddenly
Nnoo . . .

Sharon Lunga (10)
St Peter's Catholic Primary School, Stalybridge

Raven

I'm . . .
The raven
I tell people
To sing my song.
They disobey me and fight.
I take the sun off them.
I hide it for a long time
But Little Darkness gets the sun
And take it far away.
So I grab him,
Give it back,
It's there
Again . . .

Cloé Whitehead (10)
St Peter's Catholic Primary School, Stalybridge

My Life As A Football Net!

The shed door opened and the light poured in,
And two sets of hands reached in and grabbed me.
Then they dragged me out onto the pitch
Where I could see my brother on the other side,
Probably thinking the same as I was.
I could already feel the ball hit my net
And then I'd nearly fall down in agony!

The game kicked off -
But no one had scored by half-time.
With only ten minutes left in the second half,
The ball flew towards me,
So I leapt out of the way
And everybody looked shocked!

So later that day,
They took me to the dump,
And threw me in
And I was never a football net again!

Joe McDonald (10)
St Peter's Catholic Primary School, Stalybridge

The Sun

Bright
Beautifully golden,
Hottest thing alive,
Light of the world,
Glowing bright over the world,
The biggest star that ever was,
Soars high in the sky,
Lasts all day long,
Bright today,
Shine.

Robert McCarthy (10)
St Peter's Catholic Primary School, Stalybridge

The Stolen Sun

Standing boldly on my own
Shining bravely to be admired.
Suddenly darkness takes over,
Sadly my brightness has expired.
I hear beating wings overhead,
I am taken away furiously,
I finally land by being dropped twice
Then I am quickly locked up
In pure solid ice.
All my feelings start to seep out
And I weep and wail.
I'm really upset because
All my brightness has failed!
I suddenly see a shocking face,
I am left singing a beautiful tune.
I finally realise that
I am to escape soon!

Kayleigh McGann (10)
St Peter's Catholic Primary School, Stalybridge

My Life As A Blusher Brush

My life as a blusher brush,
When I look at others dipped in mush,
I feel so lucky when I'm dipped in powder,
Could her music be any louder?

When she rubs me on her face,
It feels so like a warm embrace,
It tickles so I giggle,
I love my life as a blusher brush.

Holly Sweeney (10)
St Peter's Catholic Primary School, Stalybridge

Baby Darkness

Cradled
In his
Mother's arms lay
Baby Darkness, resting very
Quietly.
Dark eyes, dark hair.
Mother knew he was very clever,
Humming the song of the raven's dream.
Long time passed and the town
Grew evil, killing animals, people fighting,
Darkness found Raven
And asked him
For the
Sun.

Lucy Sandilands (10)
St Peter's Catholic Primary School, Stalybridge

Fighting

Fighting,
Killing fish,
Arguing about anything,
Treating each other badly,
Setting people's houses on fire.
Why? thought the raven, looking down,
So he said to himself,
'I will take their sun'
His town looked
Unbelievable.

Charlotte Lees (10)
St Peter's Catholic Primary School, Stalybridge

The Ice Cream

I like it when I get to see my friend ice cream.
I don't like it when people eat me.
I'm afraid of a person who drops me on the floor
Because then I have to meet Mr Bin.
I'm happy when I meet all of my friends
Because they cheer me up.
When people eat my friend, I'd rather be a person
Because then I can eat ice cream.

Ryan Donlan (10)
St Peter's Catholic Primary School, Stalybridge

My Dozy Dad

He's so dozy
I can't compare
The time we went to Greece
He went and bumped his head

And the time I went to football
He forgot to pick me up
He arrived fifteen minutes late
But he brought me lucky stuff

We went into a gallery
He shouted out the price
Two thousand, eight hundred,
That's never right

We went into the next shop
He had an itchy nose
And then suddenly on the floor
Was loads of snot and crows.

Jordan Halliday (10)
Sir John Offley CE (VC) Primary School, Madeley

The Computer Virus

It was ICT in school
I was trying not to be a fool.
The person next to me, Miss Lee,
Was trying to get the headphones free
Her computer was all jolty
The database was quite faulty
She tried to wait just a bit
But by the end there was no wit
The whole screen was quite dead.
It began to hurt all her head
Then she went to call Miss Taylor
But this tactic was a failure.
Miss T said, 'You can move.'
Miss Taylor wasn't in the groove
Now Miss Lee wants a computer
The computer's not a tooter.
That's the end of the story
I hope it was not too bory.

Matthew Howard (10)
Sir John Offley CE (VC) Primary School, Madeley

Snow

A white clean sheet just covering the ground,
She is coming by the pound,
Slushing up and stretching out,
You don't want to hear her shout,
Falling gently through the air,
She is restless, without a care,
Landing softly melting down,
She wears a big angry frown,
Rising up and breaking through,
It is safe now, she can't get you.

James Stuart (11)
Sir John Offley CE (VC) Primary School, Madeley

What Happens Next?

Happy rain dancing about.
Doesn't know when he should shout.
As he wears a pretty silk cloak.
Jumping in a wooden boat.

Clear noise drip-drop drip.
He only takes a little sip.
As he glides in the air, he doesn't care.
It falls all day but doesn't tear.
But that's all he needs to fight a bear.

Constant knocking, when he will stop I don't know.
As he keeps tapping on my window.
Tap dancing on my roof, I've got proof.
As the sky turns dark blue, what he will do
Keep it between me and you.

Emilee Ward (10)
Sir John Offley CE (VC) Primary School, Madeley

The Big Match

We're on the way to the match
Our teacher tells us just to relax
But none of us can, we're in the footie mood
We get there in time to snack on some energy food
The match starts, we score a goal
After that Harry falls down a hole
The match goes on, we win three-nil
We manage to pay the petrol bill
And as we get back
We get off the bus,
Once we say we've won, everyone claps.

Ryan Jennings (11)
Sir John Offley CE (VC) Primary School, Madeley

The Sun

The sun wakes up with a morning smile
Laughing at the world down below
Shines brightly over the seas
Talking to a flying crow

Shouting, screaming trying to be the best
Covering miles and miles of land
Keeping us nice and warm
Reaching down his gentle hand

Making light for the world to see
In the garden or out to play
Always happy with a smile on his face
In the sky watch him sway.

Rebecca Kavanagh (10)
Sir John Offley CE (VC) Primary School, Madeley

Raining

Rain gliding in the air
Sprinting to and fro
Speeding in and out of holes
Till all the work is done
Coming to the end of day
And then comes back tomorrow
Rushing down, rushing down
Rushing down a hill
Making shapes in the air
And even in the mill
As the sun comes out to play
The rain will say goodbye
And all the children will come out to play
As they all say hip hip hooray.

Emily Parkin (10)
Sir John Offley CE (VC) Primary School, Madeley

The Snow Warrior

Creamy sludgy whipped up snow
Charging down in a raging avalanche
Sneaking around and being inquisitive to its prey
Creating a blurry atmosphere while scouting out on the front line
Planning a cunning plan on its way to attack
Sloppy dead snowmen lying dead before him
Coming to a gentle halt at the end of the journey
Then at ease falling asleep on the sleek wet surface.

James Ball (10)
Sir John Offley CE (VC) Primary School, Madeley

Snow

Mushed up snow, whiter than cream
Charging down the mountain like a white tidal wave
And then slowly coming to a halt
Covering up footprints when people walk over him
Slowly drifting from the sky
But melting faster through the night.

Kyle Dixon (11)
Sir John Offley CE (VC) Primary School, Madeley

The Snowflake

Twists slowly as it falls into a white coat
It finds the place where it should be cold but soft
It's just entered a cold world so it sits down on a chair
It covers a stone, it spreads its small body all over.

Aaron Sumnall (10)
Sir John Offley CE (VC) Primary School, Madeley

The Rain

Joyful rain dancing swiftly
Along the wet path.

Galloping away into the distance
He will not stop.

All the children laughing at him
But he just does not care.

Up he goes onto the rooftops
Tap dancing up on there.

Now the sunshine starts to rise
So off goes the rain - goodbye.

Rebecca Degg (11)
Sir John Offley CE (VC) Primary School, Madeley

My Future

What will my future hold for me?
A runner, a horse rider maybe
What will my future job be?
I would like the best for me
So what will my future hold for me?

Laila Phillips (10)
Sir John Offley CE (VC) Primary School, Madeley

Storm

The clouds were grey.
The sky was dark.
A horrible storm was beginning.
A terrible group took over all the land.
A gush of wind came rushing over
And lightning and thunder started.

Shannon Laban (10)
Victoria Road Primary School, Runcorn

The Destructive Storm

It was a dark evening as the clouds rolled in.
Then suddenly
It went very dark.
The trees swayed back and forth.
Lights danced in the air.
The frosty wind began to howl.
There was an eye-blinding dazzle as the lightning
streamed across the sky.
The thunder was like a massive erupting volcano.
Oh what a storm!
Eventually the drenching rain crashed down due to
the clouds giving way.
The weather was perilous!
The temperature was below freezing!
Hours later it began to calm down and vanish into
the night sky.
It was peaceful again.

Daniel Stanton (10)
Victoria Road Primary School, Runcorn

The Storm

Oh what a storm!
Wind howled like a wolf in danger
Lightning dazzled across the bleak sky
The wind felt bitter, wild and wintry
Trees swayed and quivered in the darkness
What would happen next?
Creatures staggered to a hiding place
The air was far from tropical
Thick fog scurried across the sky
Suddenly, the clouds separated
Had the storm stopped?

Jamie Powell (10)
Victoria Road Primary School, Runcorn

Oh What A Storm!

Oh what a storm!
A flash of light lit the sky.
Gloomy clouds gathered together.
Everything went black over the hills.
Thunder and lightning struck.
It suddenly lit the sky up.

As the rain started to lash down,
it got darker and darker.
There was a crash, bang and a crackle
then suddenly the wind swayed the trees
breaking anything in its way.

As the Earth got sadder, it got blacker.
Suddenly a cold misty breeze,
the sun began to come out.
The storm stopped.

Elle Watson (11)
Victoria Road Primary School, Runcorn

The Storm

Lightning strikes
Thunder crashes
The wind blows
Rain splashes in puddles
What will happen next?
Movement in every location
Animals sprint for safety
The ground is as soft as can be
Trees wave with fear
Lightning cuts through the sky
Thunderclouds get darker
Will it stop?
Who can tell?

Willem Green (10)
Victoria Road Primary School, Runcorn

My Storm Poem

Oh what a storm!
The wind was howling.
The tree was swaying its branches
The atmosphere was frozen.
The trees were rattling.
Suddenly there was a frightening sound.
It was the storm generating its power.
After that there was a creepy,
Humid sound of thunder in the sky.
Then the rain stopped.
It started to shine.
The storm was calming down.
The storm was finishing.
The great land was growing again.
The storm was finished.

Jake William Lewis (10)
Victoria Road Primary School, Runcorn

The Big Storm

Oh, what a storm!
Clouds turned black,
And lightning flashed,
Blowing trees down.
Thunder roared and howled.
It was cold and dark,
The sun was completely gone
It was gone forever and ever!
It was scary and frightening and sad.
An eye opened up
Light shone, everyone cheered.

Nathan Evans (10)
Victoria Road Primary School, Runcorn

Storm

The atmosphere froze
The world became a giant statue.
Trees bowed,
The storm had awoken.
A cluster of clouds gathered,
Making gloomy shadows,
Night came.
Powerful rain drenched the city,
Lightning flashed
Oh what a storm!
Thunder crashed, banged, and rattled,
Bombs exploded in the sky.
The bitter, vicious, cold wind howled,
Leaves twirled,
Diving along the street.
Lightning wriggled across the sky.
Was this storm ever going to end?

Ellie Thornton (10)
Victoria Road Primary School, Runcorn

Storm

It was a horrible evening.
The rain got worse as the day grew on.
Suddenly the clouds turned grey
Like thick dirty smoke.
It started to lash down,
The sky went black.
It flashed with lightning,
Started to thunder.
Finally, it calmed down
The clouds turned white,
The sky turned blue,
The thunder and lightning ceased.

Rachel Ward (10)
Victoria Road Primary School, Runcorn

Oh What A Terrible Storm!

The wind froze as the birds flew.
All the animals calmed down.
The sky turned gloomy and murky.
The sky looked like coal.

Suddenly there was a shot of lightning.
Trees bent down like a person grabbing something.
The floor was damp.
All the rain poured down everywhere.
The rain felt like freezing snow.
The thunder clapped.

The wind settled down to sleep.
All the smoke faded away.
The animals that were scared came out.
The sun came.
Everything was back to normal.

Sophie Hindley (10)
Victoria Road Primary School, Runcorn

Oh What A Storm!

No sun,
Gloomy clouds,
Rain splattering, sky getting dark.

Wind swirling wildly like a wild dog,
Sky blackened even darker,
Thunder roared even louder,
Lightning struck dangerously,
In the murky sky.

Oh what a storm!

Caris Spracklen (10)
Victoria Road Primary School, Runcorn

The Storm

What a wonderful view; beautiful flowers and trees.
It went silent, calm and still.
Thunder banged, crashed and rattled.
It was a deafening rumble.
A blinding flash lit the sky.
Lightning like a dazzling adder
Lightning slithered through the bleak sky.
Oh what a storm!
It was noisy, dreadful and murky.
The wind blew rapidly and destroyed everything in sight.
The rain drenched the path, then flooded grass
Everything stopped but the sky was still bleak.
Had it stopped?
Who knows?

Kayleigh Woodcock (11)
Victoria Road Primary School, Runcorn

Thunderstorm

A rumbling sound started to roll.
A thunderstorm was coming.
It was gloomy and grey
Wind swirled wildly.
Thunder rattled like a snake's tail.
Dazzling strikes of lightning flashed across the sky.
Leaves froze and raindrops smashed like stones
Flooding grids and streets.
Lightning zoomed across the sky like a shooting star.
It all went calm.

Jasmine Goldstein (10)
Victoria Road Primary School, Runcorn

The Storm

Oh what a storm,
Wind blew like an enormous tornado,
Lightning was like a racing car zooming through the sky,
Sky's tears
Thunder like a giant's stomach rumbling,
Gloomy sky like a muddy sea splashing,
Children screamed all night long,
Trees bend like they were about to snap.

Rebecca Halle (10)
Victoria Road Primary School, Runcorn

The Storm

The atmosphere was peaceful,
Suddenly the sky turned black,
A sudden dazzle of lightning pierced the sky,
As hailstones hit the ground, they shattered violently,
Wildly the wind whistled and roared,
The thunder rumbled and crashed out of the sky
Like a bunch of fireworks
Oh what a storm!

Scarlett Jazmin Stubbs (10)
Victoria Road Primary School, Runcorn

The Storm

Oh what a storm,
It banged and crashed.
Thunder was in the air,
Lightning lit the sky with bright adders,
Wild wind whipped the trees like a piece of string.
Rain lashed down like it would not stop.
It was getting colder by the minute,
A small thunder lost its way in the darkness.

Kealan Ashley (10)
Victoria Road Primary School, Runcorn

Oh What A Storm!

A sparkle of lightning
flashed across the sky.
Gloomy clouds covered the sky like a dark sheet.
Thunder growled across the world.
Colder and colder as the rain got
heavier and heavier,
crashing against the ground.
Clouds started to swirl together,
everything went black over the hills.

Kyle Kinsey (10)
Victoria Road Primary School, Runcorn

A Day At The Fair

A day at the fair,
What can I hear . . .
Roller coasters whooshing round and round,
Now that is a very loud sound.
The sound of children screaming
Piercing everybody's ears,
That is all I can hear.

What can I see . . .
Crying babies and moaning ladies,
Laughing children
Playing in the fun house building.
Everyone looking happy,
That is all I can see.

What can I smell . . .
Lovely little lollies,
And old smelly dollies.
Sticky hair gel,
That is all I can smell.

Georgia King (10)
Waterloo Primary School, Liverpool

The Magic Box

Based on 'Magic Box' by Kit Wright)

I will put in my box . . .

A tree that is shaped like a rubber,
A rubber that is shaped like a tree.
Harry Potter as fat as can be,
Scoff, scoff, scoff
The clouds are candyfloss.

I will put in my box . . .

Candyfloss clouds
Pillows shaped like pyramids
Pyramids shaped like pillows
Beer tasting like water
Water tasting like beer.

My box is made out of . . .

Big pink crinkled-up brain cells
Seven sizzling saucy sausages.

I will go with my box to . . .

Get on the plane to Gozo
Go get prezzies for my mates
Go for a shandy
Go and have a takeaway.

Lee Clarke (10)
Waterloo Primary School, Liverpool

Autumn Leaves

The leaves they are turning,
The colours look like they are burning.
Orange, red, green and brown,
Watch the leaves all fall down on the ground
We kick them around
Listening to the rustling sound.

Alex Melton (9)
Waterloo Primary School, Liverpool

Holidays

Sun burning, sunbathing sun,
Or snowboarding, ice skating fun.
Cold as an iceberg
Hot as the sun
Going on holiday today
Whoosh, whoosh, whoosh.
You are flying into space and back
With more planes starting to stack.
So climb aboard and say goodbye
And soon you will go to fly.
It starts to fly by
So don't start to cry.
'Cause you can't enjoy the sun
Or have lots of fun
Straight with the people right now
'Cause they'll come back with sunburn or frostbite
And they won't have fun for a year
So stop with the tears
And start counting years
Before it's your turn to go and vegetate.

Bronwyn Emma Richardson (10)
Waterloo Primary School, Liverpool

Beehives

Beehives are big and beehives are small,
If you try and get some honey you'll be getting to the hospital.
As fast as a bee and as slow as me,
A hive is a hive of death,
Think before you draw your last breath.
Sting, sting, sting, bees do bite, with a lot of might.
A bee will always protect the queen, I mean
Why can't there be a king?
A king is a knight with a lot of might,
You know what, bees aren't always right!

Oliver Sharman (10)
Waterloo Primary School, Liverpool

Mrs Ford

Mrs Ford is as athletic as a cheetah,
And as busy as a bee.
She's always on the go, go, go,
Her eyes are drooping stars,
She has shiny, sunny skin.
She's always kind and caring, caring, caring,
She's always lovely to me.
She is as clever as an owl
And she reads us lovely stories, stories, stories.
She wears lovely clothes,
And always crazy toes.
She's always very funny, funny, funny,
She calls us Honey Bunny
She's very colourful.

Amy Wright (10)
Waterloo Primary School, Liverpool

The Witch's Cauldron

Plop, plop, plop, in go the ingredients,
Eyeballs, slugs, snails and spiders.
Plop, plop, plop, in go the ingredients,
Bogies, old socks, toenail flickers and a dead cat.
The ingredients are a handful of death.
The witch was a cackling old devil,
She stirred with a fat chicken leg
And added a slippery, slimy snake.
She stirred it round and round,
Oops, a toenail dropped off into the cauldron.
The witch gleamed with happiness.
I snuck upon the devil as quickly as a cheetah
And shouted, 'Oops, in goes the witch!'

Lauren Burdell (10)
Waterloo Primary School, Liverpool

Winter

The wind was as cold as an ice cube,
The grass was a jewel in the morning,
I felt the chill on my shoulders as I walked.
Winter is here
Winter is here.

The wind was a chilly, cold chatter,
The trees were a rainbow of colours,
The mist was a ghost of the morning.
Winter is here,
Winter is here.

I snuggled up nice and warm,
I drank my warm hot chocolate,
In front of the telly nice and warm.
Winter is here
Winter is here.

Tiffany Gray (10)
Waterloo Primary School, Liverpool

Liverpool

L is for the Liverpool team
I is for I love Liverpool FC
V is for the new striker called Veronin
E is for exhibition matches
R is for rivals who we beat
P is for Peter Crouch who is Liverpool's top scorer
O is for an own goal which Liverpool don't do
O is for over the world people come
L is for Liverpool - victory which we have.

Matthew John Williams (10)
Waterloo Primary School, Liverpool

The Snake

The slippery, slimy snake
Is a fast snake.
He is as fast as a horse,
He sleeps all day
And eats all night.

He is as greedy as a pig,
He eats mice and rats.
It is so yuck, yuck.
I wouldn't want to meet him,
He slips and slides around.

I saw him once,
On the grass he was.
I walked off, he followed on.
I picked him up and threw him far.

Olivia Jane Morris (10)
Waterloo Primary School, Liverpool

I Met A Genie

I met a genie just the other day,
Three wishes for me,
Hip hip hooray!

I wished for shoes,
I wished for clothes,
I wished for magic and hair bows.

He took me on his magic carpet,
And we went to the moon.
We met Basil Brush,
He said, *'Boom boom!'*

My mum woke me up,
I said it couldn't be a dream.
The genie was gone,
No more wishes for me.

Megan Dodds (10)
Woodslee Primary School, Bromborough

Everyone's Best Friend

Everyone's best friend
Really is quite simple,
Absolute perfection
With no zit or pimple!

Relaxing but exciting,
An amazing stress reliever,
You really can't guess who it is,
You really don't do ya?

It's there when you need it,
Its scent is aromatic,
It can be a shape shifter,
Soft, smooth or thick.

You may think I'm a nutter
But you've already met
Everybody's very best friend
Is simply . . . *chocolate!*

Elinor Boult (10)
Woodslee Primary School, Bromborough

My Horse

Horses can be black,
Horses can be grey,
Horses can be white,
Or even light bay but . . .
My horse is chestnut.

My horse is not just a horse,
He is a friend,
I can talk to him,
He understands.

I watch him gallop,
Smooth as glass,
Gracefully,
Eventually he gallops right past.

Abigail Davies (10)
Woodslee Primary School, Bromborough

Christmas

The tree has arrived! I can't believe it's here,
It's not long for Christmas, it's getting so near.
With tinsel and baubles and an angel on the top,
We'll have a good Christmas with a bang and a pop!
Presents are stacked all around the tree,
There are some for my mum, my sister and me.
People are busy putting cards in the mail,
Even the dogs have tinsel round their tail.
Everyone's out, the shops are so busy,
There's queues everywhere and my mum's getting dizzy.
Christmas Eve is here, you know what they say,
It's really special if it snows on Christmas Day.
Turkey, roasties, gravy, veg,
I hope it's snowed, I'll be out on my sledge.
Christmas Day is here, we run down to see,
What presents are there under our tree.
My sister asks, 'How did he get all this under the tree?'
Little does she know, he has his own key.
Everything I asked for and wished for came true,
I do hope everyone gets what they wished for too!

Beth Greenwood (10)
Woodslee Primary School, Bromborough

Feelings And Animals

Red is for anger like an erupting volcano.
Yellow is for brightness like the shining sun.
Blue is for water in a flowing stream.
Green is for the lush grass.

Brown is for horses who get quite muddy.
Black is for muddy dogs.
White is for swans who swim on the lake.
And red is for foxes.

Conor Murphy (10)
Woodslee Primary School, Bromborough

There's A Mouse In The House

There's a mouse,
In our house.
It never comes out
We've seen where it's been,
But it's never about.

He scratches and claws,
At carpets and doors.
We'll have to watch out
We don't tread
On his paws.

He's ripping the sofa,
And gnawing the pipes.
He's a very big pain
And we've all had enough.

We're so frustrated
We're moving away!

Thomas Raybould (10)
Woodslee Primary School, Bromborough

Fairy Tales

F is for fairies that dance in the wind.
A is for action that heroes enjoy.
I is for ice crystal shoes that Cinderella wears.
R is for roses that the prince always gives.
Y is for yellow, the colour of fairy dust.

T is for twinkling like the stars in the sky.
A is for apple like the poisonous ones.
L is for lying, what the baddies always do.
E is for exciting, you never know what will happen.
S is for sleepy which fairy tales should make you feel.

Anya Harrison (10)
Woodslee Primary School, Bromborough

Families

Families around the world are spread out,
Whether in floods or a drought,
United they look after one another,
Cousins together or sister and brother.

Aunties and uncles flowing like water,
Nephews and nieces, son and daughter,
All around are families happy and strong,
Saying hello, goodbye, come in or so long.

Mothers and fathers, toddlers and teens,
Lots of love and the occasional screams,
Grandpas and grandmas there's lots more,
Babies, children and in-laws galore.

Half-brothers, half-sisters there's a lot,
Not to mention adopted, we never forgot,
Steps aren't left out, just saved until last,
Always remembered just like the past.

Kes Earl (10)
Woodslee Primary School, Bromborough

Night-Time Is . . .

Night-time is dreaming time,
Night-time is sleeping time,
The moon shines down at night,
The stars twinkle bright,
The sky turns black,
Night-time is quiet time.

Night-time is . . .
Bedtime!

Sophie Hawkesworth (10)
Woodslee Primary School, Bromborough

The Seasons

The flowers in summertime,
The sun in your face,
Going on lots of fun days out,
And packing your holiday case.

All the different colours in autumn,
Orange, red and brown,
Kicking all the leaves about,
Which means you're never down.

The beautiful snowy scenery in winter,
Having snowball fights,
Lots of fun and Christmas presents,
And all the Christmas lights.

All the springtime animals,
Lambs and rabbits too,
All the lovely flowers and grass,
And every cow goes moo!

Jodie Cann (10)
Woodslee Primary School, Bromborough

Christmas Time

C is for Christians that sing,
H is for holly we bring,
R is for Rudolph that flies,
I is for icicles that are so gentle
S is for Santa who brings us presents,
T is for tinsel that twinkles
M is for midnight, the magic comes,
A is for angels that listen no more
S is for shooting stars that glide.

Erica Williams (11)
Woodslee Primary School, Bromborough

School Mornings

My alarm goes off at 7 o'clock
And I can't find my matching sock.
I brush my teeth when I'm already late,
I can't wait to see my mate.

I need to get ready fast,
I haven't even had my breakfast.
Finally I'm on my way
But then I remember it's Saturday.

Liam Kearns (11)
Woodslee Primary School, Bromborough

Dance

Jump, hop, skip, swirl,
Dance around with a twirl.
Jump, hop, skip, swirl,
Dance around like a sparkly pearl.
Jump, hop, skip, swirl,
Leap in the air with a whirl.
I hope you have enjoyed my
Jump, hop, skip and swirl poem.

Anna Yates (10)
Woodslee Primary School, Bromborough

Dogs

Labradors are cute and always want to play,
Poodles are fluffy and jump around all day,
Terriers are small and have pointy ears,
Rottweilers are nice but can be pretty fierce.

Curtis Betley (10)
Woodslee Primary School, Bromborough

Dark And Scary Night

When it's dark at Hallowe'en,
All the little children are gonna scream!
I'm going to a party on Hallowe'en night,
I can't wait for all that fright.

I love the moon when it shines.
Please somebody try and give me a fright
On that exact night.

Dari-Anne Stevenson (10)
Woodslee Primary School, Bromborough

Summer By The Sea

Summer by the sea
Fills me with glee.
Bucket, spade in hand
Running in the sand.
Listening to the band
As it sounds so grand.
Happy and jolly
As I lick my lolly.

Lucy Williams (10)
Woodslee Primary School, Bromborough

Time

I can see the clock ticking,
It has always been this way.
Every second passing
Can seem to be a waste.
With a gentle tick-tock
An hour could have gone!
The day is very busy
As time never stops . . .

Katie Griffiths-Jones (11)
Woodslee Primary School, Bromborough

Hallowe'en

H allowe'en is a fun time of the year
A nd time to cheer
L ots of chocolates and
L ots of lovely little sweets
O wls flying in the street
W ind howling in the trees
E ven if you get some sweets
E ven if you trick or treat
N o people will care if you eat all the sweets.

Molly Ledder (10)
Woodslee Primary School, Bromborough

Hallowe'en

Hallowe'en is a fun time of year,
A time to stock up on sweets,
Lollies, chocolates and gum balls,
Lovely little treats.
Only spook when you're spooken to,
Wet and cold, it never gets old,
Enter the haunted house,
Even if you're scared as a mouse.
You're never too old for Hallowe'en.

Charlotte Stockwell (10)
Woodslee Primary School, Bromborough

Spooky, Scary Skeletons

Bony skeletons,
Dull and dead,
Cosy sleeping
In their coffin bed.
Midnight bell rings
They come out and play,
Their favourite game is,
Jump in the hay.

Sometimes they fight
Over who jumps first,
Oh no! I think there is going to be
A *head burst.*
Early morning,
They go back to sleep,
Not a sound to be heard,
Except the graveyard's door creak.

Aaron Dobinson (11)
Woodslee Primary School, Bromborough

Young Writers Information

We hope you have enjoyed reading this book - and that you will continue to enjoy it in the coming years.

If you like reading and writing poetry drop us a line, or give us a call, and we'll send you a free information pack.

Alternatively if you would like to order further copies of this book or any of our other titles, then please give us a call or log onto our website at www.youngwriters.co.uk

**Young Writers Information
Remus House
Coltsfoot Drive
Peterborough
PE2 9JX**

(01733) 890066

I ♥ cats

I ♥ Cats

Happy birthday from